Blue me Farm

ntury water power
n Hutton Lowcross

Paul Smith

First published in Great Britain in 2005 by
Westgate Publishing

British Library Cataloguing in Publication Data

A catalogue record for this book is available from
the British Library

ISBN (10-digit) 1-905544-00-6
ISBN (13-digit) 978-1-905544-00-4

Edited and designed by Westgate Publishing, 13 Farndale Drive, Pine Hills, Guisborough, TS14 8JD

Email: info@westgate-publishing.co.uk

Internet: www.westgate-publishing.co.uk

Preface

In 2001 a group of local enthusiasts decided to restore Blue Lake. This would be no easy task—the Lake had been abandoned in the nineteen-fifties and was now completely derelict. The pier had rotted away, the concrete spillway had collapsed and the valves were buried under twelve feet of mud.

Despite these problems the group persevered. They had already completed a related project at Home Farm—the restoration of a hydraulic hoist and a water turbine—and Blue Lake was next on the list. But they had not anticipated the obstacles and delays they would face.

Three years of form-filling and project-planning eventually paid off, and in September 2004 a team of contractors arrived on site. The mechanical diggers began dredging and within weeks the area was transformed. The muddy swamp now looked like an empty lake and the next phase could begin. In early October the volunteers were given boots, shovels and gloves, and pointed in the direction of the mud.

Between winter 2004 and autumn 2005 the Blue Lake Restoration Group spent their weekends mixing cement, clearing mud, rebuilding walls and repairing the dam. A community group built a stairway and a viewing platform at the southern end of the Lake. Others were busy in the background dealing with administration and a section on the Local Heritage Initiative website (www.lhi.org.uk).

By November 2005 most work was complete and the volunteers had finished rebuilding the brick walls that run along the edges of the concrete spillway. Blue Lake would soon be returned to its former glory.

New brick walls along the spillway edges

The connection between Blue Lake and Home Farm is not widely known. Blue Lake is an artificial reservoir designed to supply water, via a buried pipeline, to a hydraulic hoist and two water turbines at Home Farm. Both the reservoir and the equipment were installed in 1880–1.

Such installations are rare. Only five 'Williamson Brothers' turbines remain in this country, and two of them are at Home Farm. These are numbers 432 and 433; only 441 were produced by Williamsons so these two were among the last to be built.

Number 406 remains in its original position at Gayle Mill, Wensleydale, where it was installed in 1879. During its life this turbine has been used to power both an electricity generator and a joinery workshop.

Turbine number 1, the first one to be built, is on display at the Abbot Hall Museum, Kendal. This is a very different design to the later models.

Number 428 is on the Cragside Estate, Northumberland, the former home of Sir William G Armstrong. (Armstrong is thought to have built the hydraulic hoist, also of historical importance. Only one other such hoist is known to exist—this is in the Summerlea Heritage Park, Glasgow.)

Turbine 428 is dated 1881 and was used to power the first hydro-electric system in the United Kingdom. It was later used to drive a planer in the Cragside Estate sawmill. Two other Williamson turbines were installed at Cragside (numbers 395 and 431) and a further seven turbines were later supplied by Gilbert Gilkes & Co. Ltd., the company who bought out Williamson Bros. Engineers in 1881.

Thanks to the determination of the *Home Farm Hydraulic Machinery Restoration Group*, the Farm's hydraulic hoist and one of the water turbines are now fully restored. These are incorporated in the new residential conversions currently underway at Home Farm (2005).

The Granary turbine is to be retained in its original outbuilding, and this arrangement may one day enable working demonstrations.

The hydraulic hoist is in working order and will stay in its original place in the cart shed, now part of a house. The Joinery Workshop turbine, installed in a building next to the Farm house, is unrestored.

Contents

Chapter Summary

Chapter 1 Hutton Before 1850

Chapter 1 explores the ancient history of Hutton Lowcross—from the Saxon and Viking raids to the Norman Conquest, to the Dissolution and beyond.

Chapter 2 The History of Home Farm

Chapter 2 examines the evidence for a 200-year-old farm built from the ruins of Hooton Green.

Chapter 3 Industrialisation

Chapter 3 describes how Hutton's population more than doubled during the ironstone boom and its associated immigration from 1851 to 1861.

Chapter 4 Sir Joseph Whitwell Pease

Chapter 4 investigates the rise and fall of the Pease dynasty—the Quaker industrialists who changed forever the landscape of Hutton Lowcross.

Chapter 5 Hanging Stone Dam

Chapter 5 surveys Hanging Stone Dam, a reservoir built in 1880 and known locally as the 'Blue Lake'.

Chapter 6 Williamson Turbines

Chapter 6 discusses the turbines manufactured by the Williamson Brothers in Kendal, suppliers to hydraulic installations throughout the world.

Chapter 7 The Hydraulic Hoist

Chapter 7 explains the hydraulic hoist in the Granary at Home Farm—installed in 1881 by Sir Joseph Pease and used until the nineteen-fifties.

Chapter 8 Home Farm Machinery

Chapter 8 provides an introduction to the turnip chopper, oat crusher, oil-seed-cake breaker, bone crusher, sawmill and woodworking machinery.

Chapter 9 Blue Lake Restoration

Chapter 9 contains photographs of the Blue Lake restoration project and shows how it progressed between September 2004 and November 2005.

Introduction

The picturesque settlement of Hutton Lowcross has existed for centuries. For most of that time it was a quiet, rural community, concerned almost exclusively with forestry and farming. And for most of the twentieth century and into the twenty-first this again has been the case. But through the ironstone rush of the second half of the nineteenth century, as the industrialists and mine engineers moved in, the pace of life quickened and Hutton's character dramatically changed.

The rapid inflow of workers marked the arrival of new industries which were in sharp contrast with the old ways of life. From 1853 onwards, as the ironstone quarries and drift mines were dug around Bold Venture Gill and Codhill Farm, a series of industrialists built railway lines, workers' houses, water courses, embankments and culverts.

In 1853 Henry Thomas, lessee of Hutton and Codhill after his father's death in 1843, built a row of ten cottages called Wat's Row opposite the later site of the Hutton Schools.

By 1871 this row was demolished but from 1855 onwards Thomas had been selling off land in Bank Bottom Close for house-building. Initially called Thomas Street this area later became known as Hutton Village.

The Pease family, industrialists from Darlington, were involved in the area from an early stage, buying land around Hutton Lowcross from Henry Thomas and taking leases for an ironstone mine nearby. Joseph Whitwell Pease was to spend much of his life here. Through a process of gradual acquisition he eventually owned all the surrounding land and Estates. His local interests gradually shifted from the business of mineral extraction to the design of a country estate, which culminated in his building a new Hutton Hall in 1867.

The 1881 Blue Lake–Home Farm hydraulic installation provided a fully mechanised system for many laborious farming activities. It was in regular use between the eighteen-eighties and the nineteen-fifties, giving over seventy years of service before finally breaking down.

Acknowledgements

This book is dedicated to Mr and Mrs Wilkinson whose family have lived at Home Farm since 1922. Without their efforts to maintain the Farm's character much of what you see in this book might have been lost forever. They have been given much support and encouragement in this by the *Friends of Home Farm Action Group* and the *Home Farm Hydraulic Machinery Restoration Group.*

Acknowledgement is also due to the Local Heritage Initiative and the Heritage Lottery Fund who awarded a grant of £23,329 to pay for the dredging and restoration of Blue Lake. Thanks to them this local beauty spot will once again be a haven for wildlife and walkers alike.

Forest Enterprise and the Forestry Commission have provided much-needed support and practical advice to the Blue Lake Restoration Project.

Many volunteers have played an invaluable role in the renovation works and without their help these things could not have happened. The HFHMRG maintained their enthusiasm for long enough to see a 120-year-old hydraulic hoist and water turbine brought back to life, despite countless setbacks and disappointments along the way.

The Blue Lake team have spent many hundreds of hours digging in the cold, wet mud, rebuilding walls, compacting clay, clearing drains and laying concrete. They have restored an important part of our heritage.

Clive Wilson has been a continual source of technical advice and assistance in compiling this book, and I am deeply grateful for his help. He has provided both information and inspiration in equal measure.

Photographs and illustrations have been provided by Barbara Hubbard, Pam Wilson, Carole Harris, Eric Ward, Jim Prentice, J K Harrison, Ian Brown, Garth Shepherd and Clive Wilson. Teesside Archives in Middlesbrough provided access to OME documents.

Notes on Access

Blue Lake is on land managed by the Forestry Commission and is easily accessible from approved footpaths.

The Home Farm hydraulic machinery is on private property and is not available for public viewing.

List of Illustrations

Chapter 1

Hutton Before 1850

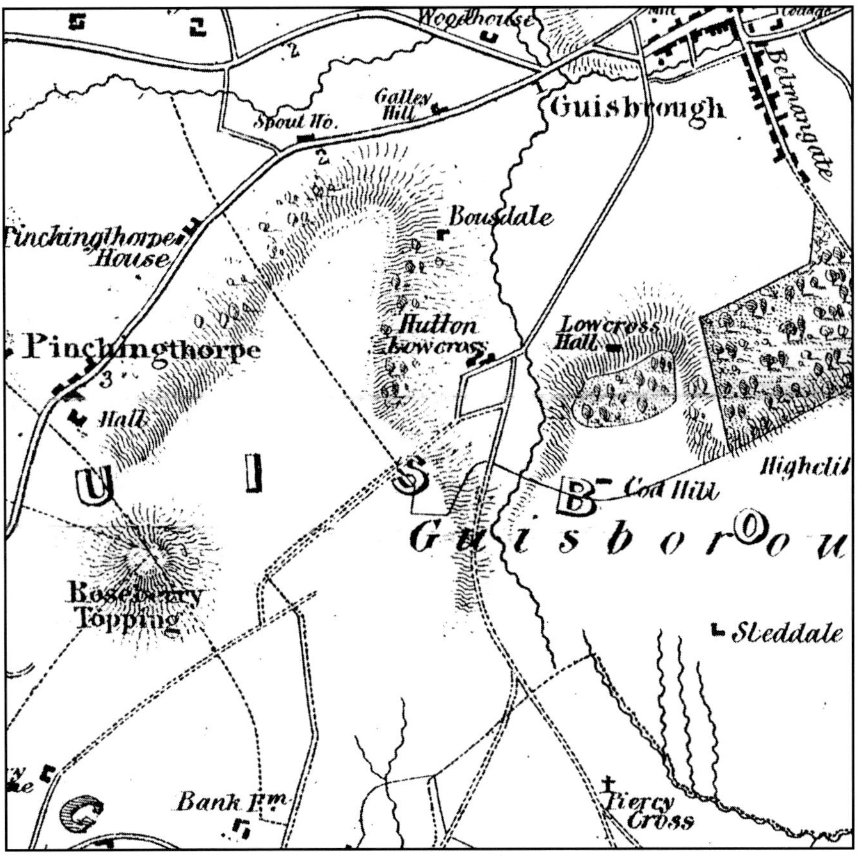

Diary of Events

AD500–800	Germanic invaders follow in the wake of the retreating Roman armies, taking over and renaming settlements with the Saxon ending '–ton' (Hutton, Ayton, Wilton, Skelton, Brotton)
800–1000	north-eastern England suffers two centuries of Viking raids
1016	England finally surrenders to the Danish ruler, King Canute. The manor of Hoton is given to Uctred, a Danish lord
1066	William the Conqueror invades England and harries the North. By 1069 the Cleveland area has been ravaged and laid waste; the land is now useless and is very sparsely populated
1086	King William's Domesday survey lists Hoton as one of three manors in Guisborough. It passes to William's half-brother
1231	the eastern section of Hoton moor is given to Guisborough Priory by Richard de Hoton; he retains the western section
1290	a document listing the possessions of the deceased Hugh de Hoton describes a water mill and 21 cottages at Hutton
1335	John de Hoton gives the manor of Hoton to Guisborough Priory but leases it back for life
1346	Nicholas de Hoton gives all his Hoton land to the Priory but remains a tenant
1408	Guisborough Priory gains possession of all Hoton land
1539	during Henry VIII's Dissolution Hoton manor is partitioned into three estates and surrendered to the Crown
1541	Hoton Hall and Hoton House are leased to Thomas Leigh
1544	Thomas Leigh dies and the Crown briefly regains the land
1547	Thomas Chaloner, now married to Leigh's widow, leases the Priory lands from the Crown
1550	Sir Thomas Chaloner purchases the Priory lands
1782	a Crown estate map shows two neighbouring settlements in the Hutton Lowcross area—Hooton Village and Hooton Green
1864	after being leased by different families over the centuries the Hutton estates are purchased by Joseph Whitwell Pease

Previous page: *An extract from an 1843 map showing the original settlement of Hutton*

Hutton Before 1850

Early History

Hutton is an ancient settlement with a written history of nearly one thousand years. Its fertile lowlands and proximity to the wooded slopes of the Cleveland hills made it a popular farming and hunting area, and created an environment that was largely unchanged until the middle of the nineteenth century.

But the discovery of ironstone in 1850 ended the tranquillity and brought railways, earthworks, terraced housing and drift mines in a massive industrial expansion.

Between 1851 and 1861 Hutton's population increased from 49 to 129.

The 1843 map at the front of this chapter shows no evidence of the mineral railways, ironstone mines or houses that would soon be built. But a quick comparison with the first Ordnance Survey map of 1856 gives some idea of the changing landscape—these thirteen years must have seen a tremendous influx of people and a period of building on an unprecedented scale.

Hutton's earlier life is unrecorded but the settlement is believed to date back to at least the Saxon invasions of the fifth and sixth centuries. Subsequent Viking raids beginning in the eighth century eventually led to Danish rule when King Canute came to power in 1016. From then until 1066 the manor of Hutton belonged to Uctred, a Danish lord. This all changed with the arrival of King William of Normandy—also known as William the Conqueror.

Documentary evidence for the existence of Hutton (then 'Hoton') begins with a reference in the 1086 Domesday book, under the heading of North Riding.

Soon after invading England in 1066 King William created a new ruling class and then began distributing land and property to his supporters. Hutton Manor was first given to William's half-brother, the Count of Mortain.

In the early twelfth century Hutton was confiscated by King Henry I and granted to Robert de Brus, but this arrangement was short-lived. Hutton quickly passed to the Thweng family then the 'de Hoton' family in a quick succession of ownership. The Hotons were associated with the manor for centuries afterwards. (The spelling was 'Hotun' or 'Hoton' until the eighteenth century when it changed to 'Hooton'. By the early nineteenth century it had become 'Hutton'.)

During these early times Hutton was a thriving hamlet tenanted by agricultural workers and servants. The lords of the manor were the de Hoton family who lived in Hoton Hall and Hoton House, close to the site of the present-day Hutton Hall.

A document from 1290, listing the possessions of the deceased Hugh de Hoton, mentions a water mill and 21 cottages at Hutton, as well as 3–400 acres of cultivated farmland. The Hutton water mill was situated at the west end of Guisborough and later became known as West Mill. It is now under the Guisborough bypass.

A small Cistercian nunnery existed in Hutton in the late twelfth century but its actual location is unknown. It later moved to a site in Nunthorpe.

Influence of the Priory

In 1119, during a period of religious revival, Guisborough Priory was built by Robert de Brus II. During the next century the church's influence grew stronger. Hutton manor remained in private ownership longer than other manors in and around Guisborough but eventually passed to the Priory.

In 1231 the eastern section of Hutton moor was given to the Priory by Richard de Hoton, but he retained the western section. Hutton Manor was finally donated to the Priory in 1335 by John de Hoton who leased it back for life. In 1346 Nicholas de Hoton relinquished all rights to Hutton but stayed on as a tenant.

Another religious institution, the Hospital of St Leonard, moved from Upsall to Hutton Lowcross during the twelfth century. Its exact location is unclear; Ordnance Survey maps refer to it as '*Lepers' Hospital (site of)*', in the area of Timber House, whereas older references suggest it was near the present Lowcross Farm. The Hospital was subsequently taken over by the Priory. Old charters describe it as a two-acre site with a church, cemetery and fishponds.

By 1408 the Priory had gained possession of all Hutton land; this was subsequently owned and managed by the Church until the Dissolution. A document from 1535, four years before the Dissolution, shows that Priory rents from Hutton were valued at £21 per year.

After the Dissolution

After the Dissolution Hutton manor was partitioned into three estates and surrendered to the Crown.

In 1541 Hoton Hall and Hoton House were leased to Thomas Leigh, the Royal Commissioner. In 1544 Leigh died and the Crown briefly regained the land—but in 1547 Thomas Chaloner, now married to Leigh's widow, leased the Priory lands (including Hutton) from the Crown, before buying them in 1550. The Chaloners continued to hold land in Hutton for several centuries afterwards.

An eighteenth-century Crown estate map (*A Plan of His Majesties Manor or Lordship of Hooton, 1782*) shows two neighbouring settlements in the Hutton Lowcross area: Hooton Village and Hooton Green. Also marked on this map is a place called Ash Close, which was an area roughly to the south of Home Farm. (Ash was a valuable timber, often planted in hedgerows. It burns well when freshly cut so was always highly prized as firewood. It is also the best type of wood for handles used on axes, picks and other tools.)

Hooton Village was not located in the same area as the present Hutton Village but in the vicinity of the later Hutton Schools. Hooton Green was a similar-sized hamlet situated near Ash Close, in the fields opposite Home Farm—the irregular surface of the fields in this area may be a clue to this long-buried settlement.

Fields to the south of Home Farm, thought to be the original site of Hooton Green

Modern Times

From 1558 until the beginning of the eighteenth century the Crown land of Hutton was administered by the Hospital of the Savoy in London. The Hospital was disbanded in 1702 but Hutton was known for many years afterwards as the 'Savoy Lands'.

The earliest surviving lease, dating from 1634, relates to Lockeres House which later became Locker House, then eventually Lowcross Farm.

By 1716 the Yoward family held the lease for Hutton Manor and in 1752 Ralph Yoward placed boundary stones on Hutton Moor. Some of his stones still survive. A condition of his lease was that Yoward would fence and enclose all woodland to protect it from cattle damage.

Ralph Yoward continued as Lord of the manor, sub-letting the Hutton farms until his death in 1781. The leases passed on in a complicated fashion until 1841 when the Crown land was reorganised. One of the more significant tenants around this time, Henry Thomas, bought Codhill Farm in 1851. Thomas lost no time in selling it on—together with mining rights—to Joseph Whitwell Pease.

It is at this time, in 1851, when Hutton began its transformation from a quiet, agricultural settlement to an industrial building site—a fate shared by many Cleveland villages.

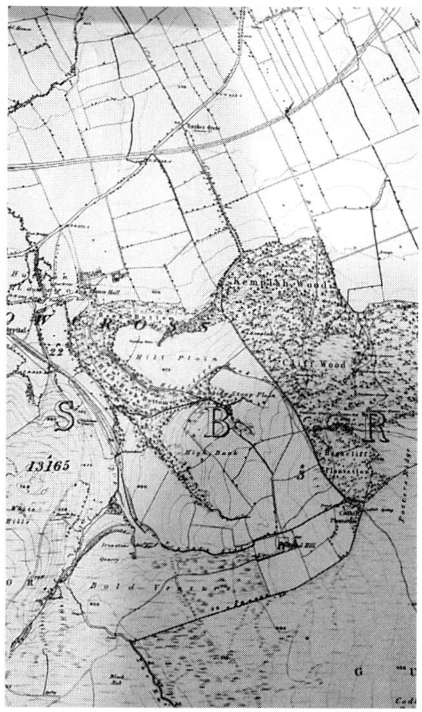

Reproduced from the year 1856 Ordnance Survey map. Changes in the landscape were caused by ironstone mining and the extension of the mineral railway up to Bold Venture Gill. The building of houses at Hutton Village began after the land was sold in 1855; consequently they do not feature on this map. The Hutton Hall noted here is the earlier, Georgian building—not the Hall built by Sir Joseph Pease in 1867

Chapter 2

The History of Home Farm

Diary of Events

1786	Richard Harding builds a house at Hutton—part of this may still exist in the right-hand part of the present house at Home Farm
1809	a deed refers to the ancient settlement of Hooton Green having been demolished and rebuilt, possibly to build Home Farm (which at this time was referred to as Church Farm)
1815	David Thomas buys out the remaining Hardings and takes a joint sub-tenancy with John Moon (the Crown still owns the land). One of David's two sons, William, occupies Home Farm
1823	David Thomas dies. William and his brother John inherit their father's leasehold farms and other property
1826	John and William Thomas add new buildings at Home Farm; the date *1826* is carved in stone above the central cart shed
1833	William Thomas dies and his brother John inherits his property
1840	Home Farm is occupied for a short time by John Bolton
1843	John Thomas dies and all his leases of Church land in Hutton pass to his only son, Henry Thomas
1844–1846	Henry Thomas's Church leases and tithes are renewed
1856	the 1856 OS map names Home Farm as *Hutton Field House*
1863	Henry Thomas mortgages his freehold land in Pinchinthorpe and his leasehold land in Hutton to Joseph Whitwell Pease
1864	Henry Thomas dies. A few years later J W Pease buys all the former Church land in Hutton from Henry Thomas's widow
1874–1881	the Farm buildings are extended and altered to accommodate the hydraulic equipment and the new farm machinery. A plan of the installation names Home Farm as *Hutton Grange*
1895	the 1895 Ordnance Survey map names Home Farm as *Hutton Hall Farm*
1902	the Pease business empire collapses; in 1903 Sir Joseph dies; in 1905 the Hutton estate is sold to James Warley Pickering
1919	the 1919 Ordnance Survey map names Home Farm as *Hutton Home Farm*; this name is used until beyond the nineteen-fifties before eventually being shortened to its present version

Previous page: *The cart sheds in 2004. The date '1826' is carved above the middle shed*

The History of Home Farm

Early References

Home Farm is at least 200 years old and has had many different names during that period. It was described as Hutton Field House on the 1856 Ordnance Survey map, then became known as Hutton Hall Farm (1895 OS map), then Hutton Home Farm (1919 OS map), before eventually being shortened to Home Farm in the late twentieth century. In earlier times it was referred to variously as Church Farm or Hall Farm. An 1881 Pease document names it Hutton Grange.

Parts of the existing buildings incorporate stone from a much older dwelling, thought to be a house built in 1786 by Richard Harding. This in turn had incorporated stone from an even older building—believed to be either the Hospital of St Leonard or the nearby Cistercian nunnery.

Two carved stones are built into a wall of the rear extension at the right-hand side of the farmhouse. This stonework is both Grade II-listed and referenced in National Monument Record F/53/95/8.

Three more carved stones are built into the western wall of the stable next to the farmhouse; these stones are also Grade II-listed and are referenced in National Monument Record F/53/93/8.

Home Farm was extended in 1826 by John and William Thomas who had the date carved into the stonework above the middle cart shed. Further buildings were added during the eighteen-seventies and eighteen-eighties.

When John died in 1843 his son Henry Thomas inherited Home Farm and other parts of the Hutton Estate.

Home Farm (Grid Reference NZ 596 143)

Site Plan

This plan is based on document U/OME 5/12 1884 in the OME collection.

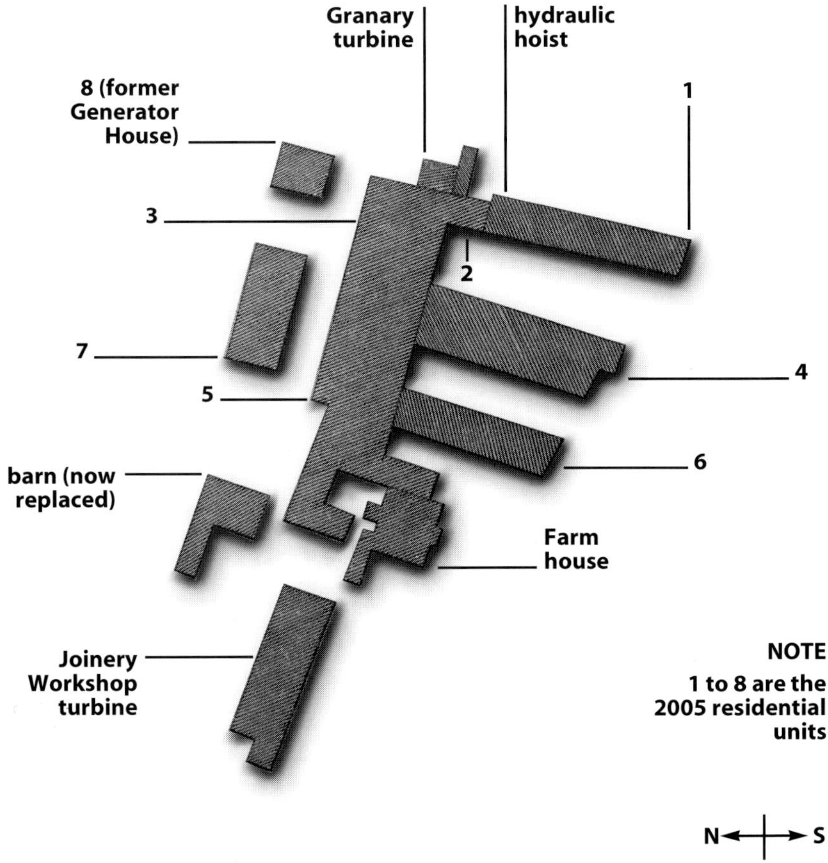

A site plan of Home Farm showing the turbines and hoist and the 2005 residential units

By 1881 Home Farm had been extended at least twice. In 1826 the cart sheds were built—these are just visible on the 1856 map (see right). Further alterations were made after the eighteen-seventies when the 'E'-shaped range of barns was added.

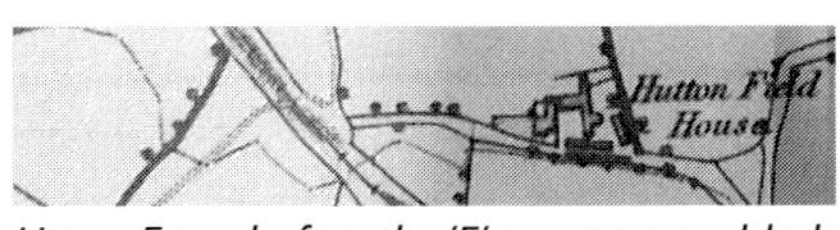

Home Farm before the 'E' range was added. Reproduced from the year 1856 Ordnance Survey map

Inventory from the 1903 auction

'Commodious Model Farm Buildings *Most conveniently arranged and all in perfect order, with water power laid on from the Estate, worked by turbine, and arranged for driving the whole of the agricultural machinery and carpenter sawing benches, thus making a great saving of labour. The Buildings comprise Cow House, to tie 14, fitted with glazed earthenware mangers, and having stone flagged floor, and dado of white glazed bricks, with Root Pulping and Mixing-House adjoining; another Cow House, to tie eight, similarly fitted; Pigeon Cote over Cow House; Calf Pen for three, Horse Box, Two-stall Stable, and One Loose Box, fitted with iron mangers and tanks, and stone paved Harness Room, fitted with grate, and having cement floor; Butcher's Shop, enclosed Poultry Yard, with stone paved causeway round, and range of Six Fowl Houses, fitted with ventilators; another Harness Room, stone paved; range of Nine Stall, lofty and well ventilated Cart-horse Stable, fitted with iron mangers and racks, stone paved, and each stall divided by iron columns, with hooks for harness; Hay House, Chaff House, Store House, Chaff House, Fanblasting House, all cement paved; stone stairs leading to Straw Loft over; Three Loose Boxes for bulls, with bricked-in Yards, fitted with mangers, with Feeding Passage leading from Root House; Mill Chamber over; and Yard, with folding gates around, which are arranged; Three Loose Boxes, with bricked-in Yards; Corn Chamber over; Two more Loose Boxes for fatting; Three Bay Wagon Shed, with Granary over; Two Bay Wagon House, with Granary over; Three Implement Sheds, with folding gates to each, and Granary over; Store House; Turbine Shed.*

Bricked yard adjacent to the Turbine Shed

Detached Generating House *Tile paved, lighted by six windows; walls lined with glazed bricks; Accumulator Room, Store Room and Coalhouse; Two Manure Houses, with folding gates, and Boiling House between; Six Poultry Houses and Yard.'*

End of an Era

The 1903 inventory on the previous page gives a sense of Home Farm in its heyday—a modern, model farm boasting the latest technologies. But the Farm was being sold off because of financial distress. The Pease family were in trouble and everything had to be auctioned to pay debts. Joseph Whitwell died later that same year.

Business continued as normal for some, though. The 1903 inventory states that *'The Joiners' and Painters' Workshops are let to Mr Edward Cruddas at a yearly rent of £2 12s. 6d., subject to three months' notice to determine the agreement at any time'*. Evidently the turbines kept on running during these difficult times.

Home Farm buildings seen from the back, shortly before redevelopment in 2005

The photographs in this chapter were taken in December 2004, a short time before redevelopment began. They provide a record of buildings that had barely changed in over a hundred years—buildings that blended into the environment yet had been a functional, practical, working farm—and a fine example of Victorian agricultural engineering.

View of the first-floor Granary with the ground-floor turbine shed visible against the wall

Home Farm—view of the single-storey block with the courtyard to the right

Home Farm—exterior view of the former Generator House

Home Farm—exterior view of the second detached building

Home Farm—inside the panelled stable

Home Farm—cattle stall and manger

Home Farm—courtyard inside the 'E' range, with the cart sheds and hoist on the right

Looking through a first-floor window towards the Hutton road, late December 2004

Planning Conditions

On 5 October 2004 Listed Building Consent was granted for redevelopment of the outbuildings at Home Farm to form eight dwellings (Decision No. NYM/ 2004/0181/LB). This was subject to several conditions, including:

'5. No works or development shall be commenced in connection with dwelling unit H2 until a report on the current condition of the machinery within the unit and a schedule of works for the repair, restoration and future maintenance of the machinery, including detailed plans, and has submitted to and approved in writing by the local planning authority [sic].'

'6. Prior to the first occupation of the dwelling unit H2 the recommendations for the repair and restoration of the machinery contained in the report and schedule undertaken in accordance with condition 5 above shall be completed. Thereafter the machinery shall be maintained in accordance with the recommendations of the report undertaken in accordance with condition 5 above.'

'7. The applicant, or their agent or successors in title shall, on receipt of a minimum of seven days written notice, permit access by the local planning authority or any specialist nominated by the local planning authority, to allow the inspection of the machinery for a maximum of four days per year.'

Chapter 3

Industrialisation

Diary of Events

1828	Joseph Pease and five Quaker colleagues form a company called the 'Owners of the Middlesbrough Estate' (the OME)
1829	the OME buys 520 acres of farmland from William Chilton. Plans are drawn up for the new township of Middlesbrough
1830	the Stockton & Darlington Railway is extended to Middlesbrough and the first house is built
1841	John Vaughan and Henry Bolckow open an iron foundry
1842	the new Middlesbrough Dock opens with space for 150 ships
1849	the Stockton & Darlington Railway is authorised to take over the dock to try and overcome competition from Hartlepool
1850	exports of coal from the River Tees are in serious decline and the future looks bleak for Stockton and Middlesbrough...until mining engineer John Marley discovers ironstone at Eston
1851	Joseph Pease and his son Joseph Whitwell Pease publish a prospectus for the Middlesbrough & Guisborough Railway—to provide a rail link from their proposed Hutton ironstone mines to the blast furnaces at Middlesbrough. They obtain a 30-year lease of the minerals (but not including jet) at Codhill in Hutton
1852	Henry Bolckow and John Vaughan open blast furnaces in Eston and Middlesbrough
1853	the Middlesbrough & Guisborough Railway is completed. Joseph Pease opens an ironstone mine at Bold Venture Gill and obtains a 21-year Crown lease to mine under Hutton Common
1857	the Hutton mines now employ 350 men and boys and reach the peak of their ironstone production: 314789 tons in one year
1859	ironstone mining in Hutton is declining—largely because of Hutton's isolated position and its poor-quality ironstone
1860	a railway incline is built in Hall Gill (adjacent to Blue Lake) to bring ironstone from the opencast mine at the top of the valley
1867	Hutton's ironstone industry is over; Hutton Hall is being built...

Previous page: *A wrought-iron bucket in the woods below Highcliff believed to be a relic from Codhill ironstone mine. This type of bucket—known locally as a 'kibble'—would once have been used to transport items into and out of the mine*

First Edition 2005

Industrialisation

Owners of the Middlesbrough Estate

In 1828, the year Joseph Whitwell Pease was born, his father (also Joseph) and five Quaker colleagues formed a company called the *Owners of the Middlesbrough Estate*. The OME planned to build a new coal port that would rival the Hartlepool Dock.

In 1829 the OME bought 520 acres of farmland next to the River Tees and drew up plans for a township called Middlesbrough. A year later, in 1830, the Stockton & Darlington Railway had been extended to the township and the first house was built. In 1842 Middlesbrough Dock opened for business.

After some initial success, trading soon became difficult. By 1850 coal exports from the Tees were declining and Middlesbrough and the surrounding areas were struggling. Fortunately the discovery of ironstone in the Cleveland hills would soon bring prosperity.

The ironmasters Henry Bolckow and John Vaughan had been operating an ironworks in Vulcan Street, Middlesbrough, since 1841, but this initially used pig iron brought in from Scotland. In 1846 they built a blast furnace at Witton Park, Durham, in order to produce their own iron, but transporting iron ore to Witton Park proved expensive.

Joseph Pease supported Bolckow and Vaughan through difficult times by continuing to buy rails for the Stockton & Darlington Railway. But by now they were desperate to find a local source of good-quality ironstone. Bolckow and Vaughan hired a mining engineer, John Marley, to investigate. In 1850, during a survey of the Eston hills, Marley discovered a 16-foot seam.

The discovery of ironstone this close to Teesside created a demand for railways, ironworks and shipping and the new ironmasters moved in. John Vaughan and Henry Bolckow set up blast furnaces in Eston and Middlesbrough, and others followed.

Over the next few years Cleveland iron became known worldwide.

Middlesbrough in 1832 (The London Illustrated News, 8th of October 1881). This farmland on the banks of the Tees saw rapid development after the first house was built in 1830

Middlesbrough in 1881 (The London Illustrated News, 8th of October 1881). Fifty years of iron production and associated industrialisation had completely changed the landscape

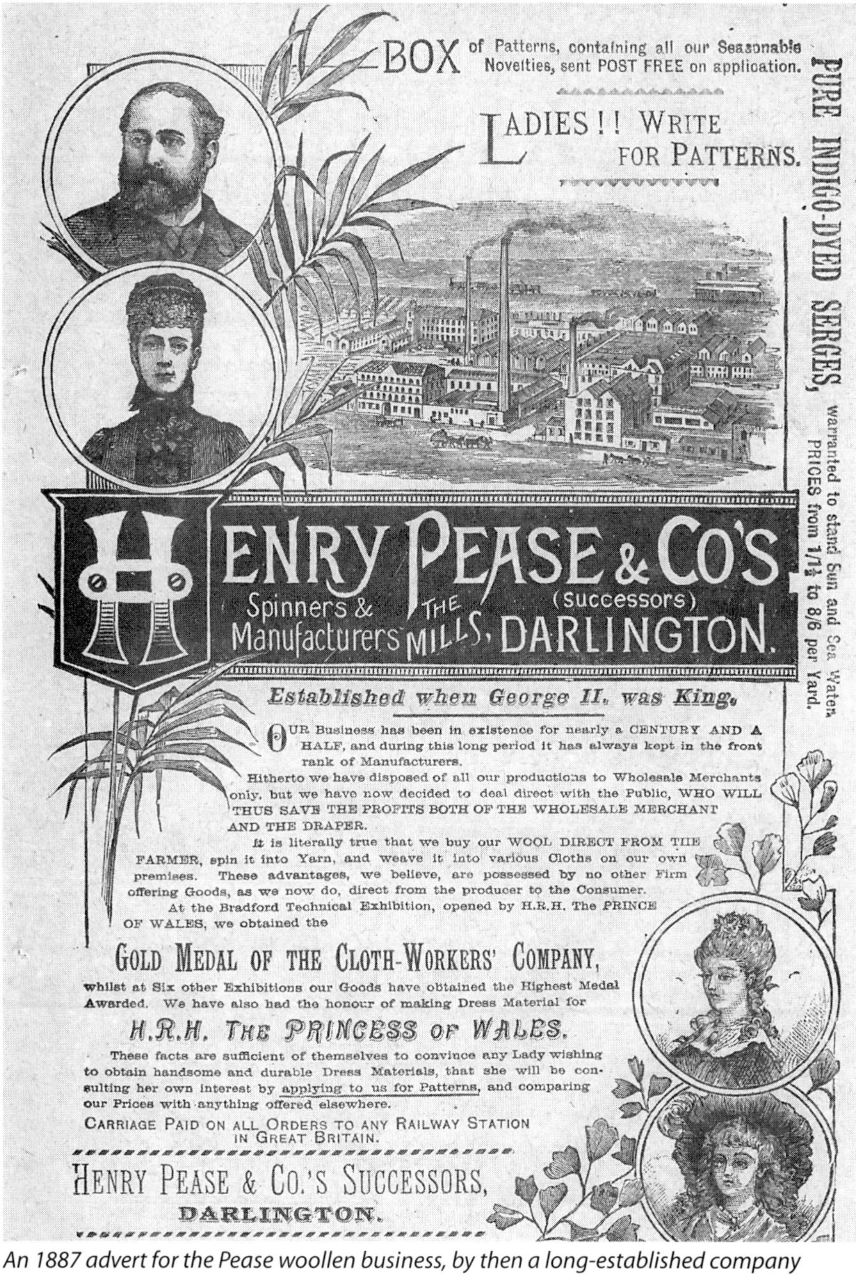

An 1887 advert for the Pease woollen business, by then a long-established company

Cleveland Ironstone

Other prospectors followed Marley's example and began scouring the Cleveland hills for ironstone. Hutton was one of the first places around Guisborough to be exploited for its mineral wealth, with Henry Thomas leasing the Codhill mining rights to Joseph and Joseph Whitwell Pease. Thomas Street (Hutton Village) was built to house the mineworkers.

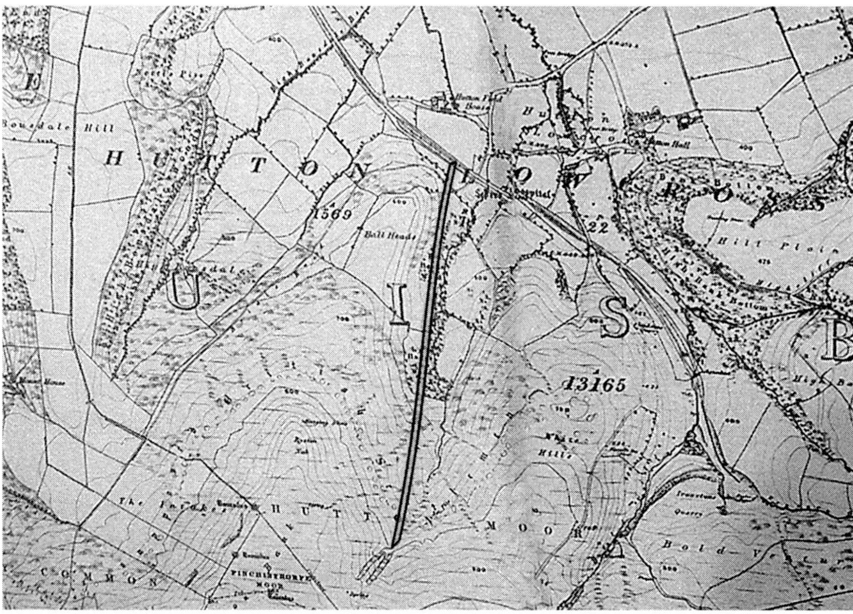

Reproduced from the year 1856 Ordnance Survey map. The ironstone quarries and drift mines of Codhill Farm and Bold Venture Gill can be seen in the bottom right-hand corner, with the mineral railway running down through Hutton and across to Pinchinthorpe. The 1860 incline railway alongside the later Blue Lake, running almost vertically in the centre of the picture, served the short-lived open-cast ironstone mine at the top of Hall Gill valley (this railway is not shown on the 1856 OS map; it is added here by the author). The three terraces at Hutton Village are not shown—construction had only just begun by this time

Henry Thomas was optimistic about the prospects of Hutton ironstone but he must have been disappointed when trade declined.

Thomas died in 1864 and in 1869 Joseph Whitwell offered to buy the estate from his widow. She refused at first but sold out three years later.

Thomas Town

In 1855 Henry Thomas sold five acres of land at Bank Bottom Close with permission from Joseph Whitwell Pease (the lessee of the Estate). The land was sold to Matthew Armitage of Darlington, a house-builder.

Armitage set up a brickworks near Bousdale House to provide the brick needed for his houses. He built only one row to start with; two more were built later, one with slightly larger houses. Their builder is unrecorded.

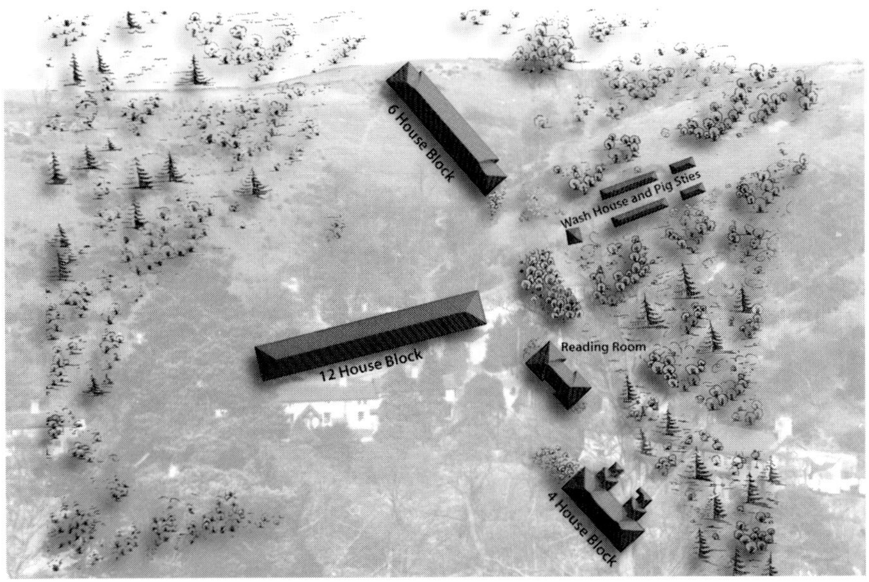

Plan of Hutton Village adapted from document U/OME 5/12 1884 in the OME collection

Before long the houses were leased to Joseph Whitwell and his sub-tenants were ironstone miners. The 1861 census shows 21 houses which means that all three terraces must have existed by that time.

In 1861 the hamlet was called Thomas Street; by 1871 it was known as Thomas Town. It was later referred to as Jet Village and the main road through was called Jet Road (jet was another mineral that put Hutton on the map: a large quantity was mined from shales above the ironstone).

By the late nineteenth century the area was known as 'Hutton Village'.

The Mineral Railways

The Middlesbrough-to-Guisborough branch railway opened in 1853 and in 1861 Hutton Lane Station was built near the present-day Highcliffe School. This was replaced in 1865 by Pease's private Hutton Gate station nearer the Hall. This was extensively altered (or possibly rebuilt) in 1895. In 1904, after the break-up of the Pease Estate, Hutton Gate opened to the public. It finally closed in 1964.

Nothing remains of the railways that carried ironstone down from Codhill and Bold Venture Gill except for some short embankments and a few field markings near Home Farm.

Perhaps the nearest resemblance to a 'railway' that was still visible in recent years was the route of the 1860 incline from the top of Hall Gill valley, running alongside the later Blue Lake. This track displayed (until about 2001) numerous large timbers laid across the track in a lateral arrangement, giving the appearance of ancient, eroded railway sleepers.

Further down the track, in the field next to the main road, a deep cutting is clearly visible. Here, at the junction of the Codhill and Hall Gill mineral lines, railway sidings were recorded on an 1862 Crown Estate Map.

The 1860 ironstone incline down Hall Gill valley, alongside Blue Lake, as it was before 2001

Chapter 4

Sir Joseph Whitwell Pease

Biography

Name	Joseph Whitwell Pease
Birthday	23 June 1828
Birthplace	Darlington
Father	Joseph Pease Esq., MP for South Durham from 1832 to 1841
Mother	Emma Garney of Lakenham Grove, Norwich, youngest daughter and co-heiress of Joseph Garney, Esq.
Brothers and sisters	Jane Emma Rachel Elizabeth Edward John Henry Arthur Francis Richard Gurney Alfred Charles
Wife	Mary Fox of Falmouth, daughter of Alfred Fox Esq., Shipping Agent. She married Joseph Whitwell on 23 August 1854
Children	Emma Alfred Edward Sarah Joseph Albert Maud Helen Blanche Lucy Agnes
Religion	Quaker
Pastimes	hunting and shooting, sea fishing, deer stalking
Titles	Sir. Baronet (1882) Member of Parliament from 1865 President of the Peace Society Chairman of the North Eastern Railway from 1894
Died	23 June 1903 (his 75th birthday) in Falmouth

Previous page: *A print of Hutton Hall from 'A Series of Picturesque Views of Seats of the Noblemen and Gentlemen of Great Britain and Ireland', by the Rev. F. O. Morris, B.A., 1880*

Sir Joseph Whitwell Pease

A Man of Influence

The Hutton Estate we see today is the legacy of Sir Joseph Whitwell Pease, a Quaker from Darlington.

Sir Joseph's grandfather, Edward Pease, made his fortune in the family woollen business before investing in the infant Stockton & Darlington Railway in 1818. This railway was initially planned as a horse-driven system but Edward decided to use the locomotives built by George Stephenson. Its success led to the rapid development of coal distribution and iron production across Durham and North Yorkshire.

Edward's second son, Joseph, took over his father's interests and added a colliery business. It was Joseph who, in 1839, offered John Vaughan and Henry Bolckow a site for an iron foundry and rolling mill in the new township of Middlesbrough.

Joseph Whitwell Pease had a long association with Hutton Lowcross, beginning in 1843 as a fifteen-year-old juror at the Manor Court of Hutton (even then an old-fashioned institution). The Manor Court was set up to deal with local problems such as encroachment. An 1843 case that Pease may have heard involved

> *'...George Aswell, a wild rough character, who had enclosed and cultivated some land bordering the Kildale road, and lived there with his daughter in a mud hut which was in 'a fearful state.'' (by Grace Dixon, in Two Ancient Townships).*

Joseph Whitwell obviously had a previous family connection with Hutton but he became more closely involved from 1851 onwards when he began mining ironstone on the Codhill estate. By the mid-eighteen-seventies J. W. Pease and Co. was the largest ironstone producer in the area, operating mines at Upleatham, Loftus, Craggs Hall and Lingdale.

The Peases were good employers who provided well for their workers.

Sir Joseph built the Mission House in 1856 and Hutton Schools in 1857. The Cottage, on the corner opposite Hutton Gate Station, was the miners' hospital until approximately 1870.

Contemporary Accounts

The following article from *Vanity Fair*, published in October 1887, gives a contemporary account of Sir Joseph Pease—by then a 59-year-old MP:

> *'The Peases are a keen and prosperous Quaker family, established at Darlington, and, when Joseph Whitwell was born nine-and-fifty years ago, had not yet recovered from the severe use of broad brims and the second person singular [the Quaker use of the word 'thou' instead of 'you']. But Joseph was as keen, and meant to be as prosperous, as any of his kin, and soon threw aside these trappings as cumbersome. At seventeen he went into the family business with his father Joseph and other partners, and at three-and-twenty took the command of it. It was then a large business, and has since become larger, consisting mainly in the ownership and management of vast coal and iron mines, which employ some five thousand workmen, and the exercise of a preponderating influence, direct and indirect, over all the railways and all the trade of Durham. With these advantages, with very great capacities for trade, and with the largest private interests at his back, Joseph naturally aspired to a share in handling politics and public interests, and was, as naturally, elected in 1865 for a Durham constituency, a part of the country for which he still sits. And, having been long a fervent supporter of the Liberal Party, he was created a Baronet in 1882'.*

An 1887 Vanity Fair caricature of Sir Joseph Pease, drawn by the artist known as 'Spy'

The article continued,

'Sir Joseph is a very excellent keen man of business. He is not however a great statesman and hardly even a prominent politician. Yet he has many of the qualities that go to push a man in the Liberal ranks. Without being immodest, he has no excess of humility, and when he speaks, which he does with authority on subjects with which he is acquainted, he speaks with much complacency and with a patronising air which invariably carries conviction to his own mind.

He deplores the convivial tastes of his compatriots for strong drink; is concerned as to the demoralising effects of the opium poppy; and, after great trouble of mind on the Home Rule question, he appears now to have settled down for good into a docile follower of Messrs. Parnell and Gladstone, for whose Home Rule Bill he voted on the occasion of its defeat.

Sir Joseph is a hale, hearty, robust man, long given to hunting with the Cleveland, and the renter of a grouse moor in the Braemar Highlands. He lives at Guisborough in Yorkshire, but has several other little places in which to lay his head. He has established science classes among his workmen. He is President of the Peace Society. He is an amiable person in private life. He is very rich'.

A portrait of Sir Joseph Whitwell Pease, 1st Bt., by Thomas Lewis Atkinson, painted in 1876 (courtesy of National Portrait Gallery)

The Hutton Estate

Following his early involvement with Hutton's ironstone mines J W Pease began to realise the area's potential as a country estate. On his early visits he stayed at Hutton House Farm, a Georgian mansion house belonging to George Reade, signing his address as 'Hutton Hall'. In 1864 he bought the whole property; the new Hutton Hall was built between 1866–1867.

By 1860 the ironstone mines around Codhill were in decline due to both their poor-quality stone and their isolated situation. Pease gave up gradually, and with reluctance, but his other mines were much more productive—particularly Upleatham mine which he took over in 1857.

Sir Joseph gradually removed all traces of Hutton's industries and beautified the estate. One of the early casualties was Wat's Row, ten cottages built by Henry Thomas in 1853 (opposite the later site of the Hutton Schools). By the time of the 1871 census these had disappeared without trace from the Hall grounds.

For the next 50 years Pease built up his estate by leasing and buying the surrounding land and farms. In the eighteen-sixties he demolished the existing (Georgian) Hoton Hall and built the new Hutton Hall.

The new Hall was finished in 1867. Designed by Alfred Waterhouse, a Quaker architect related to the Pease family, it had 38 bedrooms, exotic gardens, conservatories, cricket field, summer houses, a boating lake, boat house and parkland. Waterhouse designed many buildings including London's Natural History Museum.

In 1874, after further acquisitions, Joseph Whitwell became Lord of the Manor for both Hutton Lowcross and Pinchinthorpe. At its peak the Hutton Estate covered 280 acres, with Hutton Hall its centrepiece.

Pease 1867: bricks at Bousdale, left over from Sir Joseph's building activities

Sir Joseph's plans also involved the other buildings on the Estate. Home Farm became the 'model' farm, mechanised with the latest in water power; Hutton Gate Station was a private railway terminal for the Pease family; the Lodge was a purpose-built reception for Estate visitors; local education was provided by the 1857 'model' Hutton Schools; Hutton Village represented a fine example of workers' housing; his Stable Block had all the newest technologies; an 1890 steam-driven generator at Home Farm provided electricity to Hutton Hall and Pinchinthorpe Hall; the Estate hothouses grew bananas, peaches, grapes and nectarines.

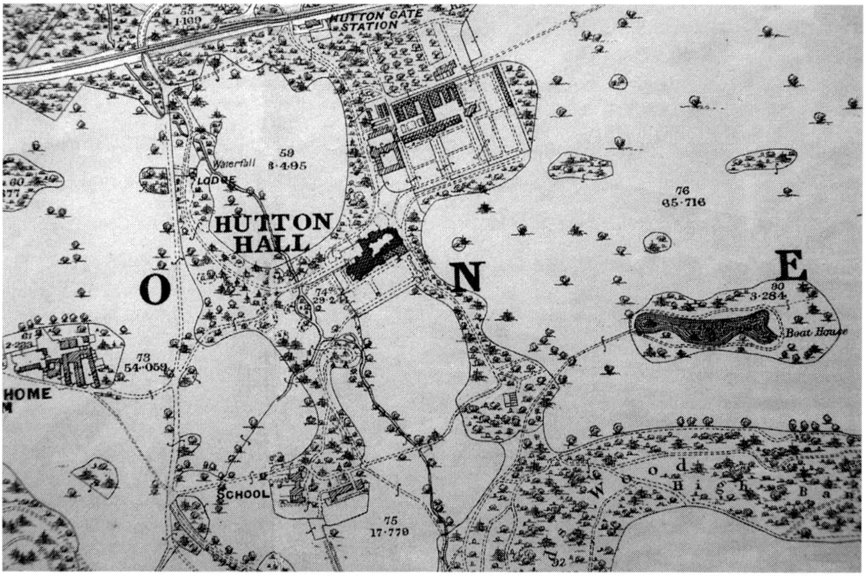

A map of Hutton Hall from 'Sir J. W. Pease's Cleveland Estates, Sale of 1903' (OME archive)

Despite the many attractions of the Hutton Hall Estate Sir Joseph spent much of his time away. He had a London house where he stayed for his parliamentary duties and his wife had a house in Falmouth. From 1865 onwards he would usually spend the first six months of the year in London with regular weekends in Hutton. During summer and autumn Sir Joseph and his family would divide their time between Scotland, foreign holidays and Hutton Hall, but still found time to support local events.

Decline and Fall

Joseph Whitwell's generation were serious about their responsibilities to others but were not as strict in their Quaker attitudes as older relatives. Edward Pease, Joseph Whitwell's grandfather, frowned on their lack of austerity and their extravagance.

Joseph Whitwell often celebrated family occasions in great style, much to Edward's dislike. In 1878, on his eldest son Alfred's twenty-first birthday, Joseph Whitwell brought 800 guests to Hutton by train. As part of the same celebrations The Avenue was planted with trees.

Sir Joseph was nevertheless both generous and highly respected. It must have been a surprise to many when, in 1902, he was humiliatingly rescued from bankruptcy.

His problems began during the eighteen-eighties and -nineties. Two engineering companies, Robert Stephenson and Co. and Wilsons, Pease and Co. began losing money; Pease had invested heavily in both companies and was liable for any losses. This also came at a time when the iron and coal industries were in recession. Other loss-making Pease enterprises—such as the woollen business—were an additional drain.

By 1890 his financial position was difficult and Sir Joseph began selling property. Despite improvements the situation remained precarious. The downfall was triggered by his niece Beatrice, Edward's daughter, who wanted to cash in her shares in the company. In order to pay her off, J. and J. W. Pease had to raise a large sum of money. Complications arose and the company ended up in court. Sir Joseph died soon afterwards.

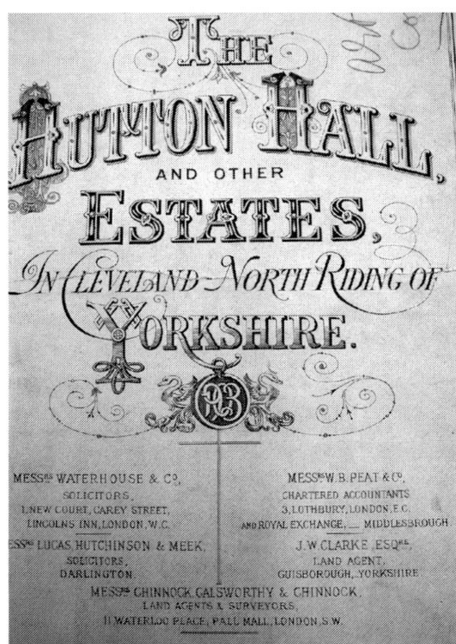

Decorative frontispiece from the 1903 sales brochure, advertising the Pease estates

Chapter 5

Hanging Stone Dam

Specifications

Location	Hall Heads Wood
Builder	Sir Joseph Whitwell Pease
Constructed	1880
Width	80 feet
Length	200 feet
Depth of water	12 feet at the deepest point (the base of the drain valve pit)
Capacity	approximately 220,000 gallons (1000 cubic metres)
Supply pipe	9.25-inch outside diameter at the dam outlet
Drain pipe	7-inch outside diameter; 6-inch inside diameter
Fall through drain pipe	15 feet from the drain valve to the stilling pond outflow
Length of drain	60 feet from the drain valve to the stilling pond outflow
Maximum flow through drain	6.5 cubic feet per second
Maximum flow through supply	15.5 cubic feet per second
Maximum spillway capacity	22 cubic feet per second Notice that this is equivalent to the combined capacity of the drain and supply pipes. This is unlikely to be a coincidence. Preliminary calculations during the planning of the Restoration Project indicated that the maximum flow simultaneously through the drain pipe and the supply pipe is 22 cubic feet per second—exactly the same as the calculated 1-in-75-year-flood capacity of the spillway. This suggests that the drain-pipe size may have been designed so that during construction of the dam it was used in combination with the supply pipe—temporarily diverted to the stream—to ensure that there was little risk of the workings being flooded. The drain pipe on its own can only cope with a flow of 6.5 cubic feet per second

Previous page: *On Saturday 16 April 2005 anyone passing Blue Lake was treated to a sneak preview of what it would eventually look like. The Lake had filled up overnight because of the heavy rains that started late on Friday 15 and continued until the morning*

Hanging Stone Dam

Archaeological Interpretations

Hanging Stone Dam is an artificial reservoir located in the forest to the south of Home Farm. Known locally as 'Blue Lake' or 'Blue Lagoon', its original name was Hanging Stone Dam because of its position below this rocky outcrop on the hills above. The water was given a blueish tinge by compounds washing out of the alum shales along the upper slopes.

No builders' plans or drawings are known to exist from the time of the dam's construction in 1880, so the following description is based on the subjective interpretation of archaeological remains. Future investigations may reveal different aspects and new interpretations.

The known facts are that Hanging Stone Dam was designed to supply water to a hydraulic hoist and two water turbines at Home Farm.

Built by Joseph Whitwell Pease, it performed a crucial role in his grand scheme of mechanisation at Home Farm. It successfully provided water from 1880–1 to the nineteen-fifties.

Hanging Stone—a rocky outcrop on the northern escarpment of the Cleveland hills

The water supply feeding the dam descends through woodland after beginning its journey on the moors.

A culvert under the adjacent track, pre-dating the dam, serves as an additional water supply. The culvert is thought to have been built around eighteen-sixty to direct water under and away from the ironstone railway incline from Hall Gill ironstone mine.

Culverts are used in other places further down the slope. One diverts water across the track near the gate. A much longer one takes the stream under the fields and across the road.

Hall Heads Wood

Hanging Stone Dam was created by damming the lower end of a natural valley in Hall Heads Wood, known variously as Hall Gill or Middle Gill.

During construction of the reservoir the valley was reworked to form an elongated 'S'-shape, with vertical wooden piles and boulders driven in to strengthen the flanks.

A layer of compacted clay was laid down to provide an impervious base, thus preventing water leaching through the bed of the reservoir.

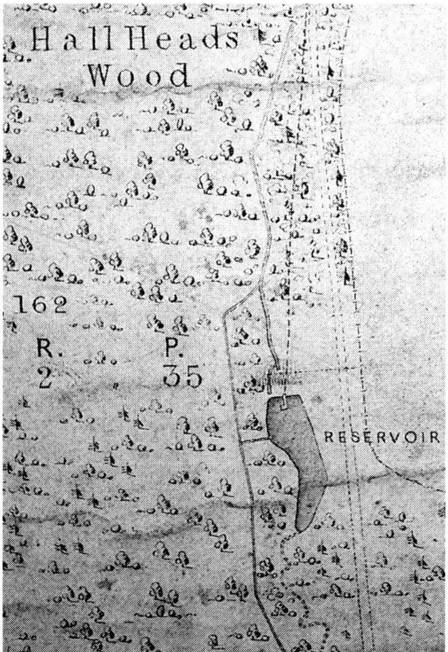

An 1874 OME map showing Hall Heads Wood and Hanging Stone Dam (reservoir)

An 1874 OME map shows the stream coming down from Haggs Wood (site of the short-lived Hall Gill mine) and entering Blue Lake. The map clearly shows that most water is diverted around the perimeter of the Lake via a bypass channel. A short channel feeds into the Lake at the northern end (nearest the dam), reducing the flow of sediment.

(References to Hall Heads Wood can be found on maps and literature from before 1867, indicating that this name existed before Sir Joseph Pease's Hutton Hall and refers instead to the earlier Hoton Hall.)

Little is known of the preparations for the scheme, although an OME document describes a proposed water supply from Bold Venture Gill, surveyed by W G Armstrong in 1871. (Armstrong is believed to have supplied the Farm's hydraulic hoist.)

The siting of the reservoir was determined by the nearest source of water that would give the required pressure, or 'head'. in this respect Hall Gill is a better location than Bold Venture Gill, being closer to the Farm—despite its lower pressure.

Sawmill Wood

Modern accounts occasionally imply a connection between Blue Lake and Hall Gill ironstone mine higher up the slope. But investigations of the literature reveal that these workings were not contemporary: Hall Gill mine was abandoned in the late eighteen-sixties whereas Hanging Stone Dam was not built until 1880.

This confusion may be due to the existence of a nearby area called Sawmill Wood, marked on Ordnance Survey maps from 1895 onwards.

Sawmill Wood (bottom right). Reproduced from the year 1895 Ordnance Survey map

It appears that a sawmill once existed nearby; in fact anecdotal evidence suggests that a steam-driven sawmill was used in this area as late as the nineteen-twenties.

Hutton woods have provided timber for centuries so it is not surprising to find references to a place called Sawmill Wood. And although the Blue Lake–Home Farm hydraulic installation was too late to be connected with Hall Gill ironstone mine, the Home Farm Joinery Workshop may have provided sawn timber and pit props for other mines.

It is quite possible that some of the timbers used in the construction of Hanging Stone Dam were reused from Hall Gill mine and its incline. Many of the wooden piles driven in to the circumference of Blue Lake have the appearance of railway sleepers, as do the timbers used in the construction of the wooden pier. Similarly the large quantities of stone and brick required for the dam may have been acquired in this way.

This 'recycling' theory is the most likely connection between Hall Gill mine and Hanging Stone Dam.

Features of the Dam

Many of the features of Hanging Stone Dam blend in well with the natural environment and are easily overlooked. These are illustrated in the drawing below; they include: 1 dam, 2 weir, 3 spillway, 4 bypass channel, 5 pier, 6 deflector, 7 cistern, 8 supply channel, 9 stilling pond, 10 outflow, 11 drain valve control, 12 sluice valve control, 13 supply pipe, 14 piles, 15 culvert.

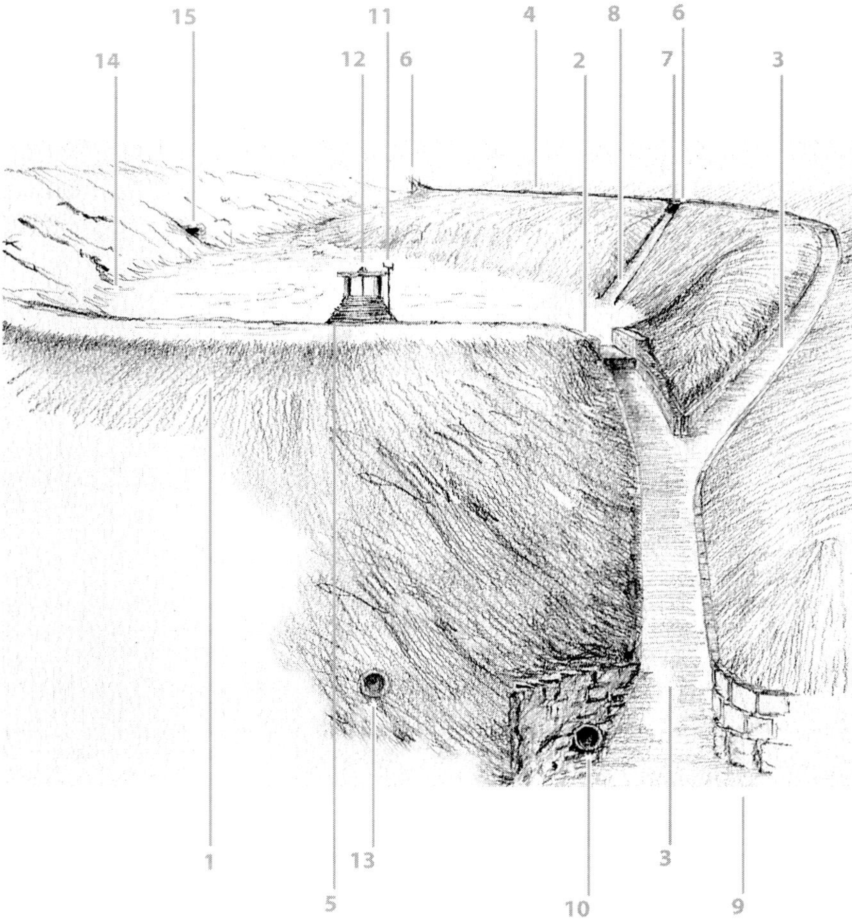

An artist's impression of Hanging Stone Dam when it was first built (Ian Brown, 2005)

Dimensions of the Dam

The diagram below shows the general dimensions of the dam.

1—500 feet as measured along the main track from the start of the dam to the deflector gate at the entrance to the bypass channel

2—400 feet from the deflector gate, along the bypass channel to the start of the concrete spillway (just above point 4)

3—35 feet from the junction of the supply channel to the dam (roughly in line with point 4)

4—100 feet from the beginning of the concrete section of the spillway to the outflow pipe in the stilling pond

5—60 feet from the weir to the stilling pond

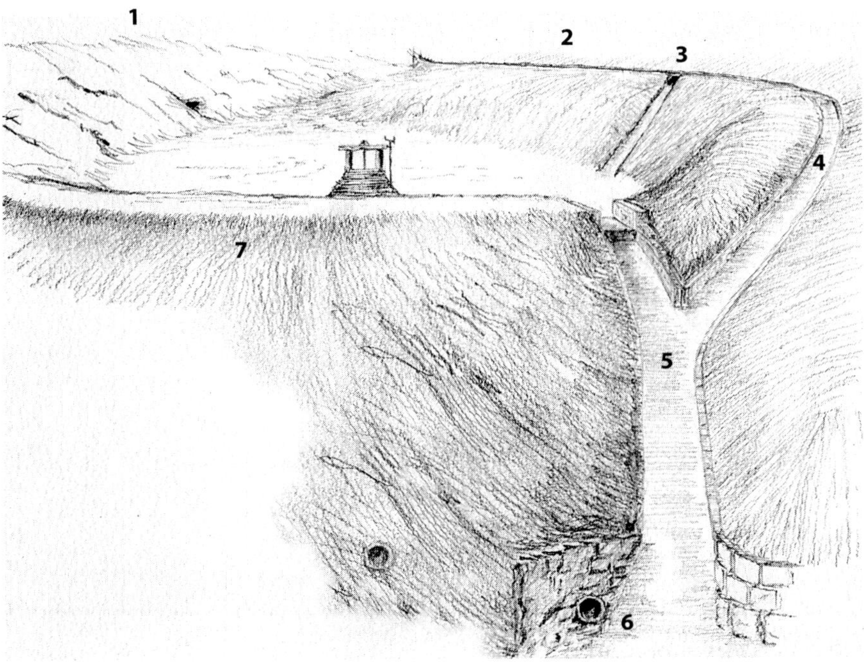

6—60 feet length of pipe from drain valve to outflow in stilling pond

7—80 feet from the main track to the opposite end of the dam

Upstream Face and Valve Pits

An artist's impression of the original dam (strainer grids not shown), Ian Brown 2005

Dimensioned Drawings

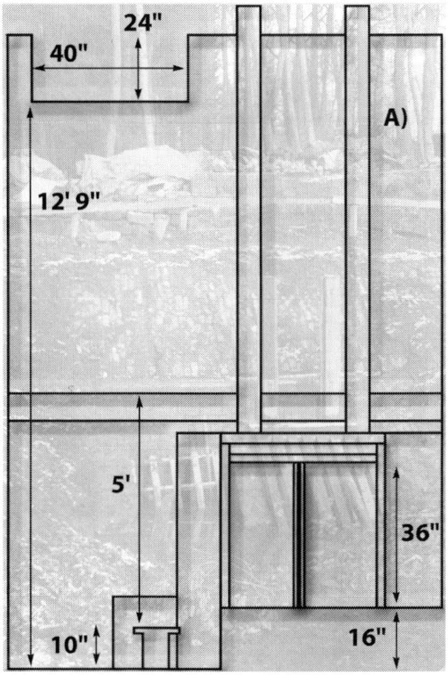

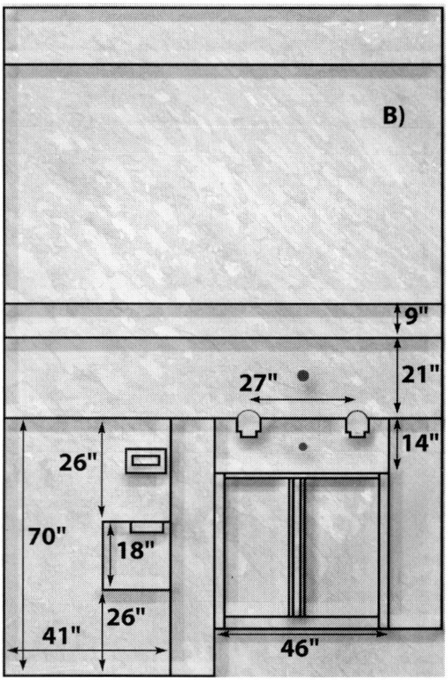

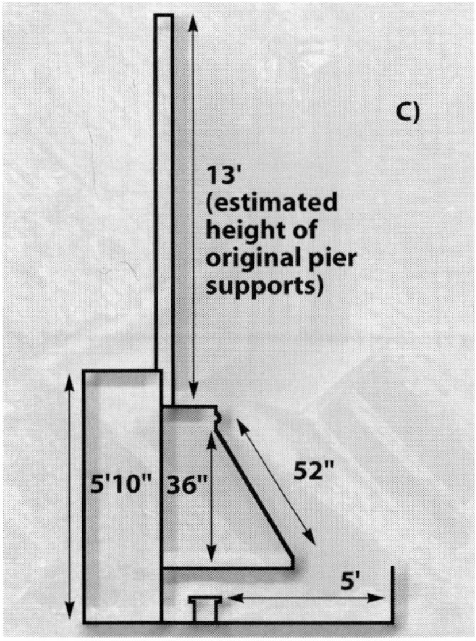

The three drawings shown here are based on sketches made during restoration in 2005. Drawing **A)** shows the front elevation of the dam; drawing **B)** shows the plan view; **C)** shows the end elevation.

The maximum depth of water is twelve feet nine inches (the distance between the base of the drain-valve pit and the weir's overflow channel).

The two wooden pier supports are estimated to have once protruded about five feet above the water level.

Pier Structure and Valve Controls

Both a drain valve and a sluice (supply) valve are built into the foundations of the dam. These were controlled by iron rods fixed to brackets on the side of the pier.

The pier was built on top of two vertical posts set in the foundations, originally extending five feet or so above the surface of the water.

Two horizontal timbers were fixed between a brick plinth on the dam walkway and the two vertical posts.

The wooden pier in 1956 (photograph by Carole Harris). The metal plate on the wooden cross-piece held a threaded rod for operating the sluice valve. The U-shaped handle operated the drain valve

Horizontal cross-pieces were laid over these two timbers to provide a strong platform that provided easy access to the valve controls.

The vertical posts are made up of two sections bolted together.

One of the vertical wooden pier supports

The front (square) section of each support descends through the brickwork into the foundations of the dam. The rear, half-round section is shorter; this is fixed on top of the horizontal stone ledge. The sections are fastened together with bolts.

Earthworks and Walls

The dam comprises two stone walls, five feet apart, rising fourteen feet from the base of the drain-valve pit to the top of the dam walkway.

The cavity between these walls is filled with impervious yellow clay to prevent water seeping through. Neither the depth nor the nature of the foundations is known.

During restoration the top of another stone wall was discovered buried under the clay. This runs from the top of the walkway, diagonally, in the direction of the stilling pond. This wall is thought to be designed to drain away excess ground water.

The two stone walls that provide the main structure of the dam. The cavity between them is filled with compacted, yellow clay

The downstream face of the dam is supported by an earthen bank rising steeply from the stilling pond below.

Downstream face of the dam showing the earthen bank supporting the stone walls

The upstream face of the dam is buttressed by a brick and stone construction containing the valve pits and the pier supports, finished with a sloping wall set at 45 degrees. This technique is unusual in dam construction and is thought to be a precaution against wave damage.

Logs are set in to the brickwork every few feet for additional support.

Piles and Supports

The eastern and western interior flanks adjacent to the dam have a brick and timber facing to provide support; these continue for several yards. In some areas of the Lake, especially on the side nearest to the track, rows of timber piles are driven in vertically and backed with large rectangular planks—presumably to prevent slippage of the bankside.

Close-up of the timber piles and supports used to strengthen the interior flanks of the Lake

The photograph above was taken a few yards from the culvert outflow.

Some of the larger horizontal timbers held in place by the vertical piles exhibit carpenters' marks—it is not known whether these timbers were reused from elsewhere.

At the southern end of the Lake near the viewing platform additional vertical wooden piles are set into the edges of the bank side. These are a long way from the main body of the Lake and their purpose is unclear.

Timber supports near the viewing platform

Weir

The weir is made from large slabs of dressed sandstone laid into a gap in the western end of the dam. Low brick walls are built on either side to funnel the water down a concrete spillway into the stilling pond below.

The weir provides an outlet for any excess water entering the reservoir, thereby maintaining the water level at its optimum height.

During restoration the internal width was widened from 31 inches to over 40 inches and the height of the walls raised by two bricks to 24 inches. This is to ensure that the weir complies with modern regulations.

View of the restored weir seen from the upstream (Lake) side of the dam

View of the restored weir seen from the downstream (spillway) side of the dam

Spillway

The spillway is a 36-inches-wide channel with a concrete base and brick sides. A short section descends steeply from the weir to the stilling pond, a distance of about 60 feet. A branch rises through the forest to join the perimeter bypass channel.

The weir spillway is designed to remove excess water from the Lake into the stilling pond below.

View down the spillway, from the branch

The photograph below shows the spillway branch where the sections from the weir and bypass converge.

View up the spillway, showing the branch

Top end of the spillway beyond the branch

The spillway becomes gradually steeper as it descends towards the stilling pond, with a maximum slope of 45% (26°) on the final section.

The spillway is concrete-lined for the first 100 feet of its length. The remaining 390-feet section through the forest is a simple clay-lined ditch.

Bypass channel

The bypass channel follows the Lake perimeter, eventually arriving at the new wooden deflector gate near some low, crescent-shaped brick walls. The bypass channel diverts water away from the stream at the top of the valley where it would be likely to collect sediment and debris.

An interconnecting channel was originally installed at right-angles to the bypass about thirty feet from the dam. This allowed water from the bypass channel to be directed straight into the Lake at times of high demand. A cistern, or pit, once existed at the junction of these two channels to provide a sediment trap. An iron deflector plate would have been positioned to send water either into the Lake or down the spillway.

In normal conditions the available water would be diverted around the bypass channel, although the map of Hall Heads Wood earlier in this chapter shows that a modest flow was retained along the route of the stream. This was perhaps to create a trickle-feed to compensate for water evaporation or seepage through the clay-lined bed of the Lake.

Iron deflector plate in the 'open' position. When the Home Farm turbines were not in use the water would be diverted down the spillway. When the turbines were running the spillway would be blocked off and all the available water diverted into the Lake

NOTE: Calculations indicate that if the turbines were running constantly the Lake could be completely drained over the course of a working day. For example, the maximum flow through the Sawmill turbine is 400 gallons per minute; the capacity of Blue Lake is 220,000 gallons; therefore the maximum operating time would be 10 hours 41 minutes, partly offset by water flowing into the Lake.

Stilling Pond

The stilling pond is an oval-shaped construction ten feet wide by twenty feet long. Stone walls on either side retain the earthen banks above and provide support for the water supply pipe to Home Farm (this pipe is buried at a depth of at least twelve inches to avoid frost damage).

The wall at the southern end of the pond, closest to the dam, contains a cast-iron outflow pipe from the drain valve. The northern end of the pond is open and discharges into the stream. The spillway enters the stilling pond at the right-hand side, close to the drain-valve outflow.

Stilling pond seen from below, showing the outflow pipe from the drain valve

The pond dissipates the energy of the water flowing down the spillway or through the drain valve outflow, reducing its impact on the stream. The base of the pond is lined with large boulders set in clay, capped with a layer of river gravel. During excavations in 2004 a wooden plank was discovered running laterally across the base of the pond, underneath the foundation boulders. Its purpose is unknown.

Drain Valve

The drain valve is installed in an open-fronted, brick-lined pit with a concrete base, twelve feet below water level. The base dips slightly towards the central area. The valve inlet is protected by a square, wrought-iron strainer box with a removable lid. An angled, hinged strainer is installed inside this box. Water enters the strainer before flowing through the valve inlet.

Drain valve (top removed) and strainer box

The valve is a cast-iron gate valve with a phosphor–bronze, screwed spindle. The valve body is set into the concrete base of the pit and is not removable. All of the internal components can be removed from the top opening of the valve, although there appears to have been an oversight in the original design of the pit: some bricks have been partially chiselled out to allow fitting and removal of the valve top.

Drain valve with top and strainer removed

The valve is operated via a spindle arrangement fixed to a pivot-and-bracket on the side of one of the vertical pier supports (clockwise to open the valve; anticlockwise to close it). The drain valve is used both to drain the Lake for maintenance work and for occasional flushing to reduce any build-up of silt in the pit. The valve outlet is connected to a 7-inch outside diameter, 6-inch inside diameter cast-iron pipe that directs water under the dam to the outflow pipe in the wall of the stilling pond.

Sluice Valve

The sluice valve is fitted in a 36-inch square, timber-lined, cast-iron box.

The back of the box incorporates a 9-inch diameter supply pipe.

Back of the valve box showing the 9-inch pipe (valve components temporarily removed)

The sluice valve incorporates a square, cast-iron plate that slides between two cast-iron runners.

Sluice valve in the 'closed' position

Rear face of the cast-iron sluice plate

The rear face of the cast-iron plate is designed to provide a tight seal.

A central spigot cast in the centre of the plate holds a forged, wrought-iron rod that connects to the valve's operating mechanism. The rod is retained in position by a bracket.

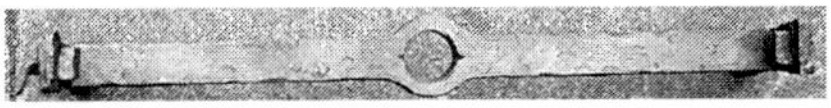

Wrought-iron rod connected to the valve

During operation the rod is raised or lowered by turning a screw on the end of the mechanism protruding from the Lake. This opens or closes the sluice valve. The picture below shows the restored sluice valve; on the right is shown a Gilkes valve.

Sluice valve in the 'partly opened' position

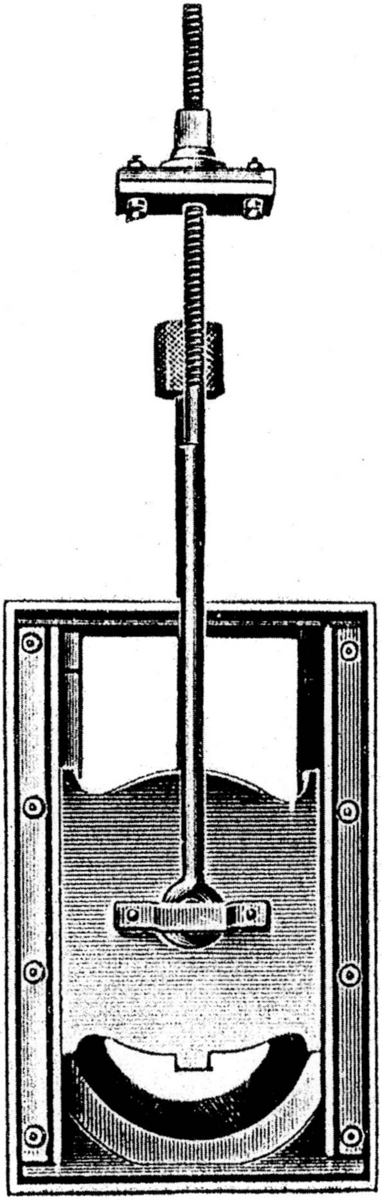

Front view of a typical Gilkes sluice valve

Air Valve or 'Rose'

An air valve or 'rose' was fitted into the pipe behind the sluice valve. This can be deduced from the existence of a small hole in the top of the pipe which is now obscured by corrosion.

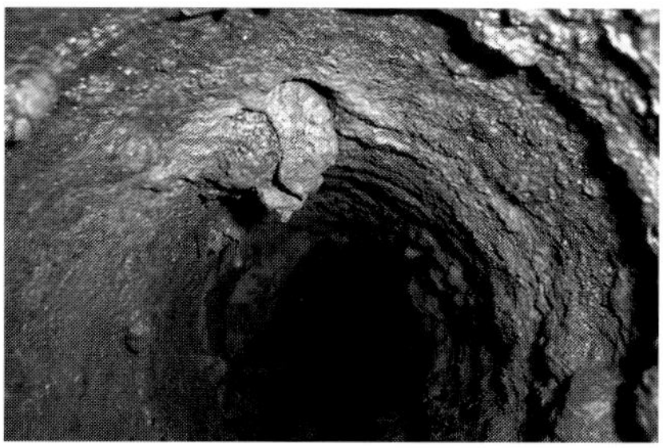

A view of the inside of the supply pipe showing the entry point for the air valve

Further evidence can be seen on the stone ledge between the pillars.

A view from above the pillars. The hole at the top is for the sluice valve control rod; the circular depression lower down in the picture is the (blocked) air valve aperture

The air valve allowed water to flow through the supply pipe by providing a means of escape for trapped air—in the same way that if you fill a straw with water then put your thumb over the end and invert it, no water will flow. When you remove your thumb the water flows.

This principle also ensures that the supply pipe will empty when the sluice valve is closed. In cold weather this is important because if the pipe is full of water it could freeze up and cause serious damage.

The air rose protruded from the surface of the water and was open to atmosphere. No remains have been found of the original pipe or rose, and photographs from the nineteen-fifties show no evidence of it.

An example of an air valve is seen in the next illustration, from a 1903 Gilkes turbine catalogue. The sluice valve illustrated is almost identical to the one used in Blue Lake—and the air pipe is in the position indicated by the hole in the stone ledge and the corroded hole in the supply pipe. (The corrosion suggests that the air valve has been missing a long time.)

Feed Pipework

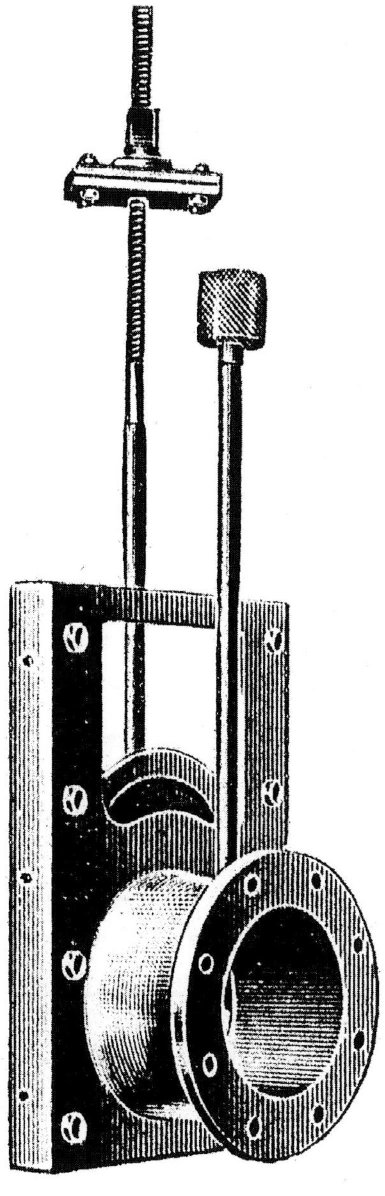

Rear view of a typical Gilkes sluice valve

A nine-inch diameter cast-iron pipe exits the back of the valve then slopes away steeply under the dam before levelling out and running at a shallow gradient through the forest.

The pipe is buried at a depth of up to three feet along its length except for a nine-feet-long section which is only half-buried; the soil appears to have been washed away because of leakage from a nearby land drain.

A section of exposed pipe in the forest

There is very little change in gradient down through the forest.

The pipe follows the line of the track then passes underground about six feet to the west of the gate.

In the vehicle turning area a land-drain manhole chamber has been built using the pipe as a foundation. From here the pipe continues for a short distance before changing direction and heading straight down towards Home Farm.

The pipe continues through the fields of the northern slope, buried at a depth of up to three feet, in line with the east-facing external wall of the cart sheds and Granary. Closer to the Farm, towards the field edge, a small cast iron cover marks the position of a stop valve—this valve isolates both the Granary and the Joinery turbine water supplies.

Upstream of this valve (the Blue Lake side) is an eight-inch spigot-and-socket pipe (nine-inch outside diameter), buried at a depth of approximately three feet. When the valve was overhauled in 2001 a large volume of gas, water and silt was released from the pipe. The gland packing was subsequently replaced.

Immediately downstream from the valve the supply pipe branches into two. An eight-inch inside diameter pipe takes a spur route to the Joinery turbine and a seven-inch inside diameter pipe continues on to the Granary turbine shed. (These pipes can be measured at the turbines; it is assumed that they are the same diameter along their entire lengths.)

A two-inch outside diameter branch pipe is taken off the Granary turbine feed to supply the hydraulic hoist. The feed pipe to the Joinery turbine directs the water sharply to the back of the Farm. The pipework in the Joinery was modified long ago to alleviate resulting water-hammer.

Investigations in 2001 revealed that the inner walls of the cast-iron pipe are corroded and the internal diameter is reduced to about five inches—if this amount of corrosion is present throughout the full length of the supply pipe from Blue Lake it will reduce the water supply to the turbines and hoist by 30–40%.

The use of nine-inch pipe suggests that the turbines were not intended to run simultaneously: a larger pipe would have been necessary for this.

Chapter 6

Williamson Turbines

Technical Specifications

	Williamson turbine 432	Williamson turbine 433
Location	basement in Joinery Workshop	lean-to shed outside Granary
Function	to drive a bandsaw, an external grindstone, two circular saws, a lathe, and (in later years) a planing machine	to drive a grain mill, an oil-seed-cake breaker, an oat crusher, a straw cutter, a turnip chopper and a bone mill
Model	Hobleys	Exhibition No. 1
Date	1881	1881
Manufacturer	Williamson Brothers, Canal Foundry, Kendal	Williamson Brothers, Canal Foundry, Kendal
Design	double vortex with horizontal shaft	double vortex with horizontal shaft
Supply	80 feet head from Blue Lake	80 feet head from Blue Lake
Pressure	35 pounds per square inch at the inlet	35 pounds per square inch at the inlet
Isolation	8-inch cast-iron gate valve	7-inch cast-iron gate valve
Inlet	8-inch outside diameter horizontal cast-iron pipe	7-inch outside diameter horizontal cast-iron pipe
Outlets	two 5-inch outside diameter cast-iron pipes discharging vertically into a 7-feet-deep drain pit below the turbine	two 4.5-inch outside diameter cast-iron pipes discharging vertically into a 7-feet-deep drain pit below the turbine
Consumption	64 cubic feet (400 gallons) per minute	54 cubic feet (337 gallons) per minute
Speed	982 revolutions per minute	1150 revolutions per minute
Regulation	four movable internal guide blades controlled by a hand-lever and chain arrangement fixed to the turbine casing	four movable internal guide blades controlled by a geared rod rising vertically to the first-floor Granary workshop
Power	7 horsepower	6 horsepower

Previous page: *Williamson turbine 433 in the Granary outbuilding, fully restored and in working order. Photographed in December 2004 before Home Farm was redeveloped*

Williamson Turbines

The Kendal Connection

By 1881 the Pease empire was at its peak. The Hutton Estate was well established and it provided an impressive setting for visitors and family alike. But Sir Joseph was still open to new ideas and was always keen to use the latest technologies.

His acquaintance with another Quaker industrialist, Gilbert Gilkes, led to the scheme of mechanisation at Home Farm. In 1881 Gilkes bought Williamson Brothers, an engineering firm in Kendal, who manufactured and supplied water turbines to hydraulic projects all over the world.

Gilkes and Pease knew each other through the Quaker community and both had connections in Kendal, Darlington and Middlesbrough.

The Home Farm Joinery Workshop turbine has a nameplate on its side casing, embossed with the words

Williamson Bros. Engineers, Kendal

—although the firm at that time would have been known as Gilbert Gilkes & Co. Ltd. They are still trading today as Gilbert Gilkes & Gordon Ltd.

The Williamson Bros. nameplate on the casing of the Joinery Workshop turbine

Williamsons manufactured 441 water turbines between 1856 and 1881, when they sold out to Gilkes. Their turbines provided power for sawing, milling, pumping, electricity generation and farm machinery.

A popular misconception is that the Home Farm turbines were part of a hydro-electric installation—in fact the electricity generator at Home Farm was driven by a steam engine. Puzzlingly, though, a gap in the wall of the Granary turbine shed lines up with a corresponding gap in the wall of the Generator house—suggesting a capacity for either the turbine to drive the generator or the steam engine to drive the barn machinery.

Customer Specifications

The diagram below shows a page from the Williamson Brothers 'works order book' containing details of turbines 432 and 433 that were supplied to Home Farm. Column 1 is the production number; column 2 is the rating in horse-power; column 3 is the specified water supply in feet-head; column 4 is the name of the customer (in this case, J W Pease); column 5 is the turbine type (in this case a double-vortex); column 6 is the type of guide blades (either fixed or movable); column 7 is the casting pattern (432 is a *Hobleys*; 433 is an *Exhibition No. 1*); column 8 is the water consumption in cubic feet per minute; column 9 is the diameter of the inlet pipe; column 10 is the diameter of the two outlet pipes.

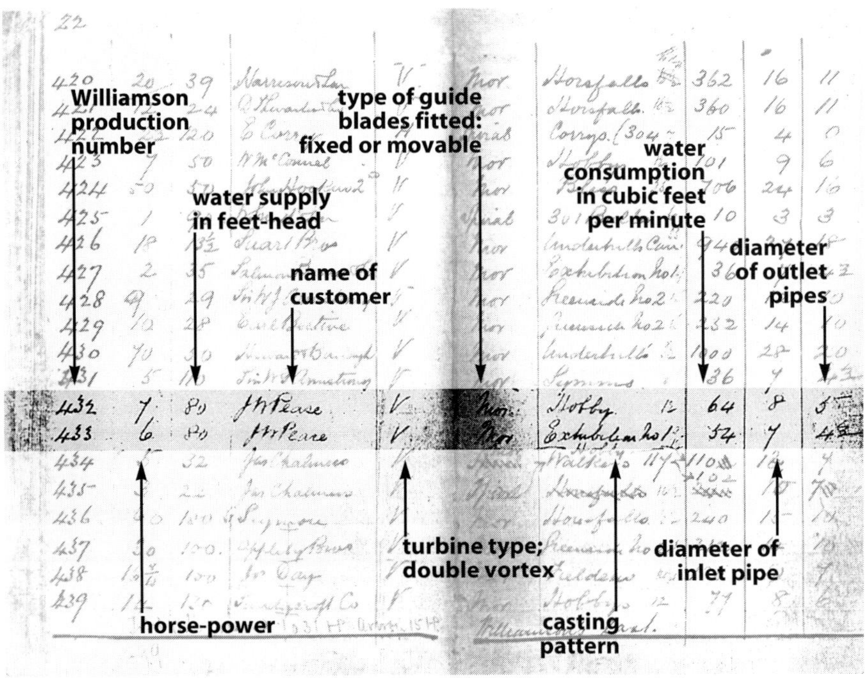

A page from the Williamson Brothers works order book listing turbines 432 and 433

Williamsons produced more than twenty different turbine castings, each being designed for a particular purpose or customer. A casting type would afterwards be known by the name of the original customer or the installation. This can be seen in the columns in the order book that give both the name of the customer and the casting type. Some examples are: Wilsons Case; Peels Case; Crappers Case; New; Wise & Leonards; Regents Canal; Stott Park Case; Horsfalls Case; Mahoneys; Fieldens Case; Underhills; Walls; Smarts Case; Routledges; Bliss; Inglis Jones; Haughton & Thompson.

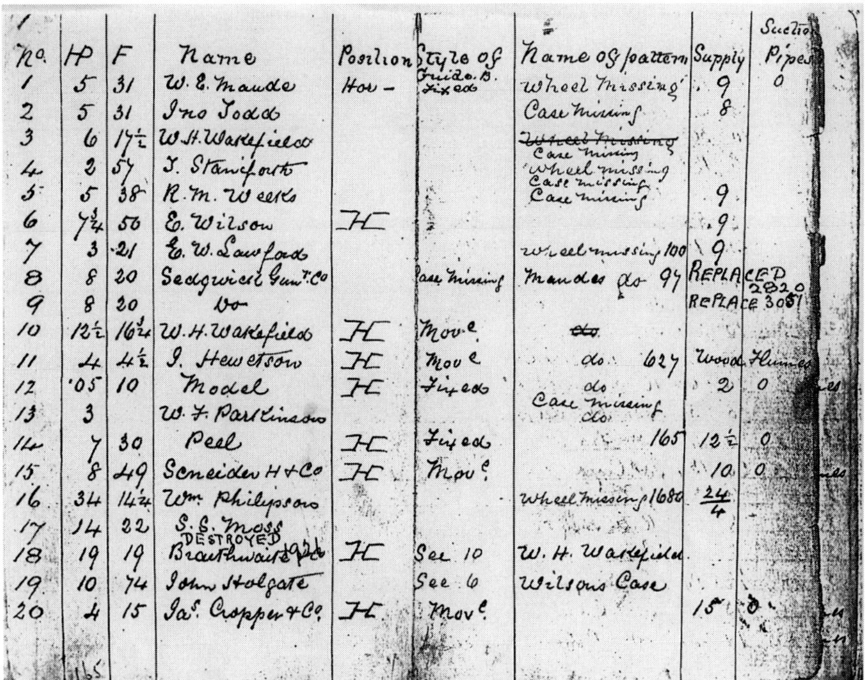

No.	HP	F	Name	Position	Style of Guide B.	Name of pattern	Supply	Suction Pipes
1	5	31	W. E. Maude	Hor –	Fixed	Wheel Missing	9	0
2	5	31	Jno Todd			Case missing	8	
3	6	17½	W.H. Wakefield			~~Wheel Missing~~ Case missing		
4	2	57	J. Staniforth			Wheel missing		
5	5	38	R.M. Weeks			Case missing Case missing	9	
6	7¾	56	E. Wilson	H			9	
7	3	21	E. W. Lawford			Wheel missing 100	9	
8	8	20	Sedgwick Gunt. Co		Case missing	Maudes do 97	REPLACED 2820	
9	8	20	Do				REPLACE 3051	
10	12½	16¾	W.H. Wakefield	H	Move	~~do~~		
11	4	4½	J. Hewetson	H	Move	do 627	Wood Flumes	
12	·05	10	Model	H	Fixed	do	2	0
13	3		W. F. Parkinson			Case missing do		
14	7	30	Peel	H	Fixed	165	12½	0
15	8	49	Scneider H & Co	H	Move		10	0
16	34	14¼	Wm. Philipson			Wheel missing 1680	24/4	
17	14	22	S. S. Moss					
18	19	19	DESTROYED Braithwaite & Co 1924	H	See 10	W. H. Wakefield		
19	10	74	John Holgate		See 6	Wilsons Case		
20	4	15	Jas. Cropper & Co.	H	Move		15	0
	165							

First page of the Williamson Brothers works order book showing their earliest turbines

The Joinery turbine, number 432, is first listed as a *Hobleys* on page 8 of the Williamson works order book. On page 11 someone appears to have misspelled the casing as *Hobbys*. By page 12 it becomes *Hobby* and then it is listed as *Hobby's* on page 18.

Both the apostrophe and the *s* come and go over the years until Sir Joseph buys his *Hobby* turbine in 1881. The Granary turbine, number 433, is an *Exhibition No. 1*. This may have been designed as a showpiece for an important industrial event.

Turbine Technology

The Williamson Brothers (Henry and William) began making turbines in 1856 at the Canal Iron Works, Kendal. They used a design called a *vortex*, patented in 1850 by Professor James Thomson, the brother of Lord Kelvin.

The vortex turbine was efficient, easy to control, and could produce a high torque at a relatively slow rate of revolution. The illustration below shows a vortex turbine with its outer casing removed, showing the wheel.

A typical vortex turbine illustrated in a 1903 catalogue from Gilbert Gilkes & Co., Ltd.

The 1903 Gilkes turbine illustration shows the internal arrangement of the vortex water wheel. In this example water enters through the top of the turbine and forms a 'vortex' in much the same way as water swirls as it goes down a sink. The design of the wheel is critical.

Water is directed onto the wheel by guide blades which can be either fixed or movable. Movable blades allow the turbine's water supply to be regulated. Waste water exits via a hole in the front of the casing then discharges through a suitable pipe.

A typical vortex water wheel (Gilkes, 1903)

The Home Farm turbines are of the *double vortex* type, in which the water wheel is split into two. Waste water discharges via separate pipes.

The following illustration shows the Granary turbine's guide blades.

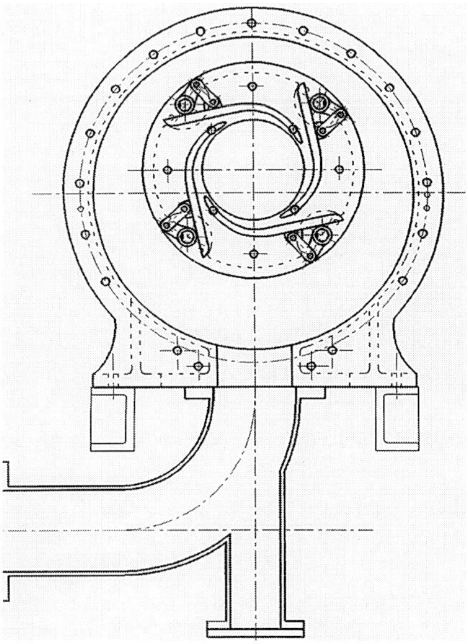

Granary turbine interior (Garth Shepherd)

Water enters the Granary turbine via a horizontal pipe and discharges vertically through two drain pipes.

The inlet and outlet pipes could be either horizontal or vertical; this does not affect the turbine's performance.

The Granary turbine is designed for a maximum water consumption of 54 cubic feet per minute; the Joinery turbine for 64 cubic feet per minute. Sixty-four cubic feet is 400 gallons—this volume would fill a four-feet-square tank every minute.

Granary Turbine

In 2001 the Granary turbine was dismantled and fully restored by the voluntary Home Farm Hydraulic Machinery Restoration Group.

The rest of this chapter contains photographs taken both before and after restoration, and extracts from the volunteers' restoration diary.

Granary turbine before restoration (photograph by Jim Prentice)

The restored turbine and inlet valve fitted with a modern pressure gauge, December 2004

Turbine Pit

The turbine pit is approximately seven feet deep and acts as a drain for the discharge pipes. Water exits the pit through a drain in the floor.

The unrestored turbine pit (Jim Prentice)

Turbine pit from above (Jim Prentice)

During restoration the base of the valve pit was dug out and lowered by four inches to simplify the refitting of the pipework.

At the bottom of the pit was a stone slab, eighteen inches wide by twenty inches long, which provided some support for the valves. The rest of the floor was made up of rubble.

The restored turbine pit viewed from above

An additional pipe discharges into the turbine pit from the hydraulic hoist in the cart shed.

This pipe runs below the floor from the hoist drain pit to the turbine pit.

Inlet Valve

The incoming water is isolated and controlled by a seven-inch gate valve and a butterfly control valve.

The isolating valve has an internal groove in which the gate slides, and the body has a set of internal brass seals on one side. The valve relies on water pressure to seal it.

A lead-run socket-and-spigot joint is used to join the pipework a few inches upstream of the valve.

The inlet gate valve and the spigoted joint. A pressure gauge was installed on the pipe to check that the Blue Lake supply was off

The butterfly control valve and its operating lever seen from above the pit

Six bolts were fitted on each valve flange; all these bolts were severely corroded. The bolts were removed using a portable grinder, blowtorch and hammer. All bolts were replaced with new ones and the flanges were sealed with rubber gaskets.

Close-up view of the valve flanges (right)

The inlet valve is operated by a removable, taper-fitted, double-ended lever that was formerly used to operate the valve at Blue Lake. Many years ago an extension piece had been fitted over this lever to allow the valve to be operated from the Granary window, in much the same way as the guide blades. It is believed that this spindle did not fulfil its purpose as it could not be reached from the first-floor window.

Turbine Casing

The turbine casing was externally corroded but generally sound. The interior surfaces had a build-up of corrosion and deposits. The rate of internal corrosion could, in future, be reduced by draining the turbine after use, so during restoration a drain tap was fitted to the bottom plate on the inlet pipe—although this was not in the original design.

The turbine casing seen from the non-drive end showing the bolts fastening the two halves

The drain tap could be used in conjunction with the existing air-bleed pipe to dry out the turbine when not in use. The drain tap would also help to prevent frost damage.

When the two halves of the turbine were separated the main seal faces were found to be lead-run. This suggests that the faces may have been damaged at some time.

Turbine Shaft

The turbine shaft was corroded and seized up at the bearings on either side of the drive pulley. To free them off, the thrust-bearing assembly at the non-drive end of the shaft was removed and the gland follower and bearings on either side of the turbine were pulled out of their housings. (The packing material was found to be greased string.)

The bearing caps on the plummer blocks were removed, allowing the shaft to be lifted slightly at the drive end, and the rust in the bearings was flushed out with oil. Considerable wear was evident in these bearings.

Plummer block bearings on the drive pulley

In the slurry removed from the turbine pit an old brass oiler was discovered. This fitted the oil-feed hole for the main gland and bearing assembly on the drive-shaft side of the turbine. (The oiler on the non-drive-shaft side of the turbine was already in its proper position when the restoration work began.)

Drive-shaft gland and bearing assembly

Glass oil reservoirs would have originally been fitted on all three plummer block bearings. These were missing but as work proceeded a bottle was found at the entrance to the first courtyard. Moulded on one side of the bottle were the words

THE NEEDLE LUBRICATOR,
REGISTERED TRADE MARK

the other side displayed the words

LIEUVAIN'S PATENT, ENGLAND

In use the lubricator bottle is designed to be filled with oil and fitted with a cork, through which a hollow needle slowly feeds oil to the plummer block bearing surfaces.

Disassembly of the turbine was performed from the non-drive end.

The turbine seen from the shed doorway. The drive-shaft exits the casing on the right; the non-drive end is seen on the left

The discharge pipe was removed first, to gain access to the guide blade control mechanism, before removal of the main shaft began.

The main drive-shaft bearings and pulley

Removal of the main drive shaft involved sliding off the drive pulley which was keyed to it. The pulley had been damaged in the past and a great deal of heat and physical effort were required to move it.

The pulley was found to be held in place with a single woodruff key.

With the pulley loosened off the two thrust collars at the drive end were easily removed. The position of the outer one is determined by an unusual collar-and-key arrangement that appears to have been designed to allow the installers some flexibility in setting up the distance between the turbine and frame to which the drive-end plummer blocks are fitted.

Even with the pulley removed the shaft could not be withdrawn without removing the lower halves of the plummer block bearing shells. These are located in the plummer blocks by pegs. To gain the necessary clearance between the shaft and the bearing shells, the drive-side gland follower and bearing assembly was withdrawn from the turbine casing. This allowed the shells in the two outer plummer blocks to be removed.

The inner plummer block was unbolted and removed in its entirety, finally allowing the main turbine shaft to be removed.

(There is a small, square aperture in the turbine shed wall, just below the window, about one-foot square. Its purpose is to allow enough clearance for the main turbine shaft to be withdrawn during maintenance. The Joinery Workshop turbine, which is installed below ground level, has a similar facility provided by a buried length of pipe.)

When it was inspected, the turbine shaft was found to be perfectly straight but was badly corroded and worn. The portion of the shaft that fits inside the turbine also displayed some corrosion.

The shaft was overhauled by a specialist engineering company before being reassembled.

During reassembly the turbine shaft was aligned to within a few thousands of an inch at five separate points along the shaft. To achieve this tolerance the bearings at the three plummer blocks were left undisturbed and the turbine was re-shimmed to match their alignment.

(An interesting discovery was made here: the plummer blocks had previously been adjusted using hardwood shims. These shims have now been replaced with brass.)

Measurements were first taken of the existing position of the end of the feed pipe, to within 1/32". The thickness of the existing gasket materials was also recorded and replicated. A rubber gasket had been used between the supply pipe and the turbine, suggesting that this was not original. The other gaskets were generally a red-lead-and-string combination. The pipework also had to be reassembled in the correct position otherwise the turbine drive-shaft would have been misaligned.

The reassembled turbine shaft and gland

To ensure that the measurements were meaningful required a lot of rust to be removed—from the beams supporting the turbine, the face of the feed pipe, and the turbine feet and inlet flange assembly.

The measurements were as follows:

- The face of the feed pipe flange that bolts to the turbine was found to be horizontal and 7/16" below the top of the beams that support the turbine.
- The two beams were found to be level with each other.
- The flange was equidistantly spaced between the beams, with a 4 3/4" gap on each side.
- The distance from the flange to the brick wall on one side of the pit was 14 13/16", and to the stone (or concrete) block on the other side of the pit was 9 5/8".
- The flange on the underside of the turbine was 9/32" below the turbine feet.

Some of these measurements were unexpected: either the pipe had dropped slightly after it was disconnected from the turbine (despite numerous supports) or the rubber gasket between the inlet pipe flange and the turbine was a minimum of 5/32" thick.

Bearing in mind that some lead packing was found under two of the turbine feet (pieces of lead sheet had previously been used as shims when the Granary turbine was mounted on its two supporting joists), it would have been even thicker, and become compressed as corrosion built up on the face of the feed pipe flange. The feed pipe was therefore replaced in a slightly higher position to reduce the thickness of the gasket.

The drive shaft, plummer blocks and pulley

Guide Blades and Control Rods

The brass linkages to the four guide blade control rods were in good condition but the levers on the ends of the rods were corroded. These were removed after drifting them along the shaft to allow the woodruff keys to be removed. The levers had to be refurbished.

The main control rod is of a softer steel than the other three rods, which appear quite hard. The hardness of the steel may explain why the level of corrosion is lower than expected. The lobes on all four rods were evidently forged from the parent metal, suggesting that they are the original parts.

Guide blade control rod seen from above

On the main control rod it appears that a mistake was made when machining the keyways: there is evidence that an extra keyway was machined and has been filled in.

The internal linkages and three of the cast-iron guide blades had been replaced with cast-brass items in the early twentieth century and were good enough to be reused. The one remaining cast-iron guide blade was in a reusable condition.

Guide blade control lever assembly

During disassembly dents were noticed in some of the iron castings. It was only when the volunteers tried to separate the components that they realised these dents had been caused by engineers experiencing the same problems in the past.

Turbine Vortex Wheel and Drive Pulley

The turbine's vortex wheel was in good condition but the sealing ring on the drive end had become detached. The method used to free off the seized bearings, although successful, may have caused this. A safer method would be to unbolt the discharge pipework from both sides of the turbine before removing the bearing caps from the plummer blocks at the drive end of the shaft.

The drive pulley suffered from impact damage during its removal; pre-existing marks show that similar damage had occurred in the past.

Vertical discharge pipe on the drive side

Turbine pulley and shaft (top of picture)

View showing the vertical discharge pipes

Joinery Workshop Turbine

Turbine 432 in the basement of the Joinery Workshop is the more powerful of the two, and differs from number 433 in several ways.

The casting is a *Hobleys*, different than the *Exhibition No 1*. Turbine 432 also has a different arrangement of supply and discharge pipework.

The unrestored Joinery turbine 432 (photograph by Jim Prentice)

The Joinery water supply is more complicated than that used in the Granary. It incorporates a gate valve, a weighted safety valve, an air bottle and a butterfly valve. These are believed to be later additions fitted to reduce water-hammer. (During operation of a turbine it is essential to avoid creating water-hammer, as this could damage the pipework.)

View of the right-hand side of the Joinery turbine (Jim Prentice)

The additional pipework and valves fitted to alleviate water-hammer (Jim Prentice)

The weighted safety valve (Jim Prentice)

Air bottle and access ladder (Jim Prentice)

Looking into the turbine pit (Jim Prentice). Williamson Brothers nameplate is partly visible

The Joinery Workshop is not part of the current redevelopment and will remain undisturbed for now.

Joinery Workshop lineshaft (Jim Prentice)

Guide blade controls (Jim Prentice)

Chapter 7

The Hydraulic Hoist

Technical Specifications

Manufacturer	unrecorded, but believed to be Sir William G Armstrong, Elswick Works, Newcastle-upon-Tyne
Date	unrecorded, but believed to have been manufactured and installed in approximately 1881
Design	a double-acting hydraulic cylinder made from two cast-iron pipes joined end to end, containing a cast-iron piston
Operation	direct-acting hoist (the full water pressure is applied to the piston)
Hoist weight	eight hundredweight (half a ton)
Stroke	11 feet (3.35 metres)
Cylinder bore	eight-inch outside diameter; six-and-a-quarter-inch inside diameter
Piston type	four inches long, cast-iron, with machined grooves externally
Hoist purpose	to lift grain and feed sacks from carts in the cart shed up to the first floor Granary for storage
Supply pressure	80-feet-head from Blue Lake
Inlet pipe	one-and-a-half-inch diameter iron pipe branching off the main 7-inch water pipe from Blue Lake
Drain pipe	one-and-a-half-inch diameter iron pipe discharging into the pit from a control valve, exiting the pit via a clayware drain pipe
Typical load	four hundredweight (two, two-hundredweight grain sacks)
Maximum load	ten hundredweight (assuming 100% efficiency and no loss)
Water consumption	three-quarters of a gallon per second (45 gallons per minute) with a typical four-hundredweight load
Rate of rise	several inches per second (depending on inlet valve setting)
Preventive maintenance	to reduce internal corrosion when not in use, the piston must be coated with a calcium-based waterproof grease and parked at the top of the cylinder. Both drain taps must be kept open

Previous page: *The top of the hoist cylinder after restoration, showing the new steel piston rod. This photograph was taken in December 2004 shortly before redevelopment of the Home Farm buildings began. The hoist had by that time been overhauled and restored to full working order by the Home Farm Hydraulic Machinery Restoration Group*

The Hydraulic Hoist

Granary Mechanisation

The hydraulic hoist was installed in 1881—around the same time as the two water turbines—as part of the Home Farm mechanisation. It is built against the rear wall of a cart shed adjacent to a flight of stone steps.

The cart shed below the first-floor Granary; the hoist is on the rear wall, out of view

The hoist could lift two grain sacks simultaneously through a wooden trapdoor to the first-floor Granary.

Top of the hoist cylinder before restoration (photograph by Jim Prentice)

This chapter is mostly based on diaries and notes written during restoration of the hoist in 2001. Additional information is provided by sectional drawings produced during an earlier survey, reproduced by permission. Most photographs were taken in late December 2004.

Hoist Arrangement

The illustration below shows a cross-sectional end elevation of the hoist.

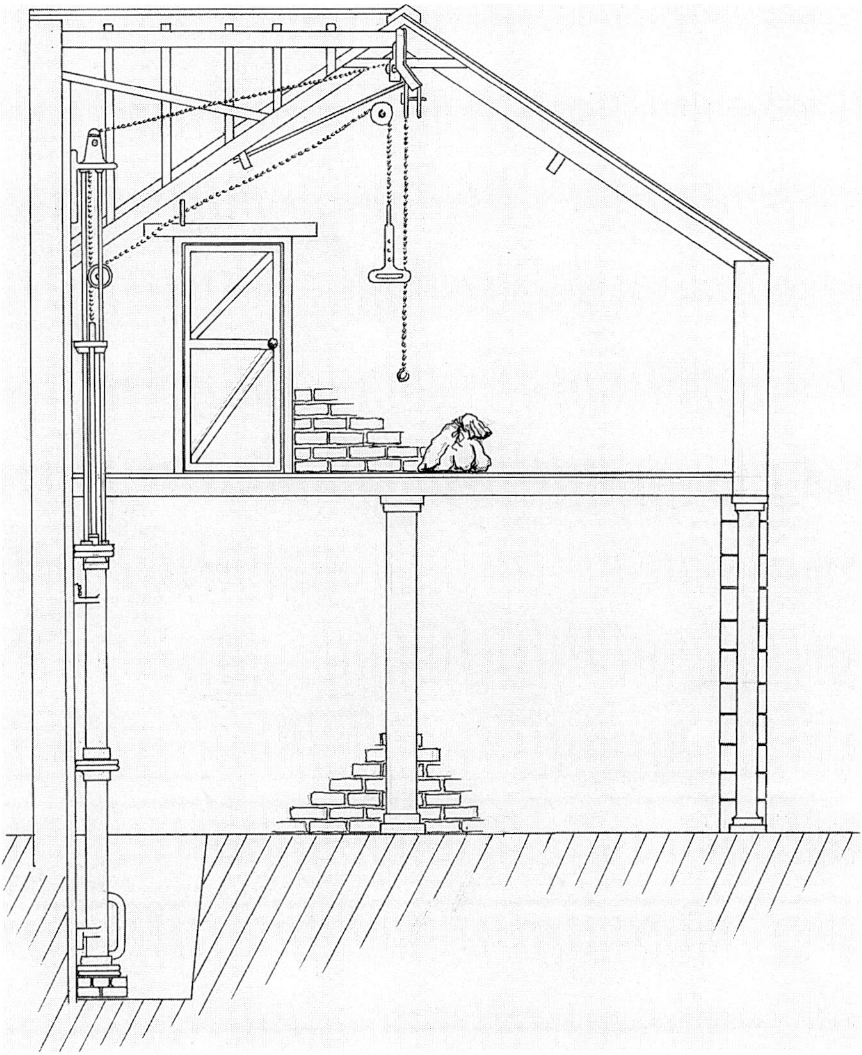

End elevation: a cross-section through the cart shed showing the hydraulic hoist. Prepared from field work survey by J K Harrison and reproduced by permission. Originally used to illustrate ***Hydraulic machinery at Hutton Home Farm near Guisborough, The Cleveland Industrial Archaeologist****, No. 25 (1998), p29–42. Adapted here by Ian Brown*

This illustration shows a cross-sectional front elevation of the hoist. The valve pit, control rod and lever assembly can be seen to the right of the cylinder.

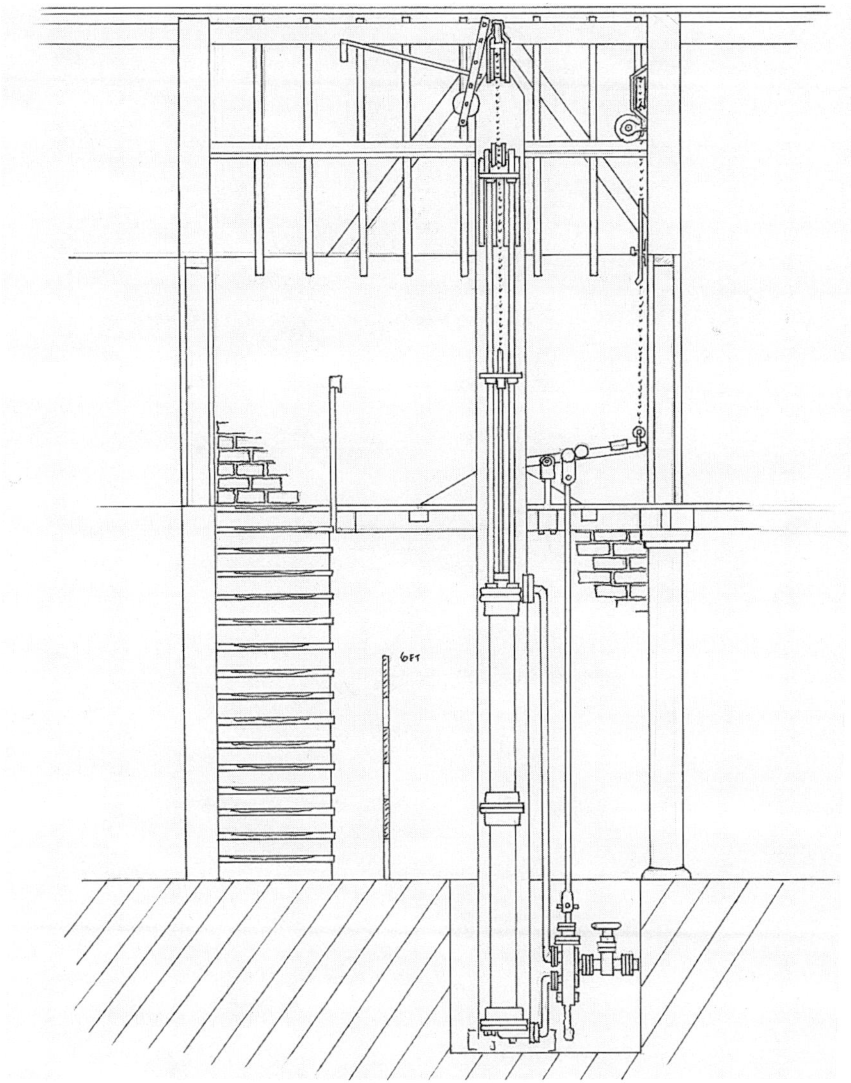

Front elevation: a cross-section through the cart shed showing the hydraulic hoist. Prepared from field work survey by J K Harrison and reproduced by permission. Originally used to illustrate ***Hydraulic machinery at Hutton Home Farm near Guisborough, The Cleveland Industrial Archaeologist****, No. 25 (1998), p29–42. Adapted here by Ian Brown*

Mounting Board

The hoist cylinder is mounted on a hardwood board fixed to the wall by three pairs of 20-inches-long bolts. This board enables the cylinder to be secured to the wall in a flat, vertical position, thus reducing the risk of cracking (cast iron is quite brittle and is likely to fracture under stress).

Upstairs the board was solid but downstairs it was rotten because of water leaks and general dampness in the hoist pit. (By the nineteen-fifties, near the end of the hoist's working life, water leakage from the piston-rod gland had become so bad that a sheet of corrugated iron was fixed in place to deflect water towards the wall, away from the grain sacks.)

Bricks had at some time been placed under the bottom of the cylinder for additional support, probably as a result of the mounting board having rotted away.

Initially it appeared that the rotten mounting board had allowed the cylinder to move: the bottom set of cylinder brackets was only half an inch from the wall, whereas the gap at the top was two inches. Also, the length of exposed thread on the bottom pair of bolts was no more than on any of the others. It was subsequently discovered, however, that the bottom set of bolts had been fitted with one-inch spacers on the outside of the wall.

The engineers who installed the hoist must have realised that the wall was uneven and decided to plane the mounting board to provide a flat, vertical surface. This would explain the variation in width at different points along the board.

A plumb line and laser were used to check that the centre points of the top and bottom of the cylinder, and the position of the chain where it passes through the bracket on the gable end, were in a straight line and vertical. The alignments were found to be perfect—unaltered since 1881.

During restoration the front face of the new mounting board had to be finished so that the six mounting points were aligned to within a sixteenth of an inch over a top-to-bottom distance of eleven feet. A traditional adze tool was found to be useful for shaping the surface of the board that bears onto the brickwork.

Cylinder and Piston

Externally the cylinder was in good condition but the piston rod was corroded. The piston was seized and would not move, even with three cwt on the chain.

Front of the hoist cylinder seen from the ground floor

To loosen the piston oil was poured into the cylinder and left to stand for a week. Both the piston and the cross-head that slides on the piston-rod guide bars were then successfully freed off.

The next task was to remove a cast-iron bracket from the first-floor gable-end wall.

This bracket secures the top of the piston-rod guide bars and has a pulley mounted on it for the chain running between the top of the piston rod and the hook that is attached to the grain sacks.

The nuts securing the bracket were removed, fortunately without having to hold the bolt-heads on the outside wall: these are two storeys high, close to electricity cables.

The bracket (which weighs about one cwt) was lifted slightly using ropes then eased off its bolts and removed.

Two pieces of lead sheet were found between the bracket and mounting board, presumably fitted to align the bracket and cylinder. On the rear of the bracket was a chalk sketch of the cast-iron spreader plate which is fitted underneath the exterior bolt-heads.

The piston-rod guide bars that run from the top of the cylinder to the bracket were then dismantled, along with the cross-head. Finally the cylinder head, the piston rod and piston could be removed.

The cylinder head was found to have a machined lip that fits into a recess, ensuring that it is fitted concentrically in the end of the cylinder. The piston was a reasonably tight fit in the bore.

The piston is a casting with half-round grooves machined into it, a similar design to that used in the hoist control valve. The piston was worn on one side to about the depth of the grooves but was suitable for reuse; a calculation of water leakage into the cylinder indicated that even under a 4-cwt load the piston would rise by only one inch per second.

Removing the piston from the rod proved difficult. The piston has a cup-shaped depression in its top, and the piston rod has a similarly shaped boss forged onto it. The cup in the piston appears to have been used as a 'former' when forging the boss, creating an extremely tight fit.

The hoist cylinder was restored in-situ because of its weight (eight cwt). It was grit-blasted to remove surface corrosion and the lower half cleaned out to remove rust and debris.

Two brass drain taps are fitted in the lower end of the cylinder—one on the bottom and the other about six inches above it. When the piston is 'parked' in the bottom position the taps can be opened to drain water away from either side of the piston.

The upper portion of the hoist showing the piston rod guide bars and cross-head

The cylinder had to be lifted a fraction of an inch to enable the mounting board to be replaced.

To prevent damage to the first-floor joists a cross-braced square of scaffold was placed against the wall.

One side of the square was placed above the cylinder and then lifting equipment used to take the weight.

During reassembly the first-floor cast-iron bracket was refitted and the piston-rod guide bars reinstalled.

Chain pulleys in the ceiling. The chain in the foreground is fixed to the top of the piston rod. It travels over two pulleys before descending through the trapdoor to the cart shed below

The lifting chain was reconnected to the top of the new piston rod and cross-head and an attempt made to move the piston up and down.

Unfortunately it stuck due to localised corrosion in the cylinder. To avoid dismantling the hoist again the piston was lowered to its bottom position, oil was poured in through the upper drain hole and the piston raised to the point where it stuck.

The assembly was then rotated while oil flowed from the top of the piston into the corroded area. Within an hour or so the piston was running freely up and down in the cylinder.

Feed Pipework

The internal pipework is one-and-a-half-inch, thin-walled with parallel BSP threaded or flanged fittings. One of the pipe elbows was a modern replacement; rubber gaskets appear to have been used when this was installed. The remaining screwed fittings are unlike modern ones and are believed to be original. Much of the pipework is thought to have been replaced at some stage.

The flanges are probably original. Most were sealed with red-lead and two turns of string. One of them had cracked across a bolt-hole. Many flange bolts were so badly corroded that it was impossible to tell whether they had square or hexagonal heads.

The feed pipework and screwed fittings were generally corroded due to their location in the damp hoist pit or close to the cylinder. The pipes would have been regularly soaked by leaks from the piston-rod gland.

The isolation valve was found to be operational. When it was first opened water escaped through numerous rust holes in the pipes. Upstream of the isolation valve the pipework was badly corroded. The outside diameter of the pipe had increased from one-and-three-quarter inches to three inches. This led to concerns about the risk of flooding until it was established that the upstream valve in the main eight-inch feed pipe was closed; this meant the seven-inch main could be safely drained into the turbine pit.

Externally the pipework is one-and-a-half to two-inches diameter, connected to the Blue Lake supply by a seven-inch T-piece. The T-piece is fitted with a blanking plate drilled and tapped to take the two-inch pipe; this is mounted horizontally, eighteen inches below ground.

Trees growing above the pipe had recently been cut down (2001) and the stumps removed using a JCB. In spite of the considerable force required the pipe was not damaged.

The pipework below ground was generally less corroded than inside the building. It comprised screwed sections of two-inch pipe with long radius bends joined by sockets. No rust holes were evident but the pipe wall was very thin. There was no sign of paint on any of the pipework.

Hoist Pit

The hoist pit contains the lower end of the cylinder, the feed and drain pipework, an isolation valve and the three-position bobbin control valve.

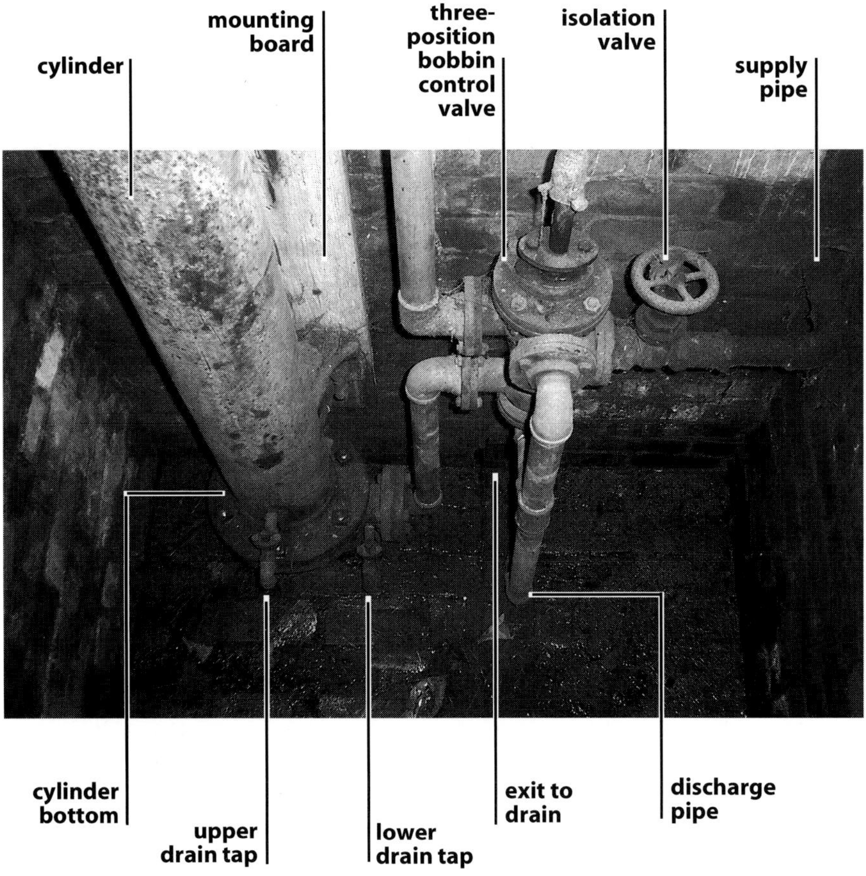

Hoist pit containing the feed and drain pipework, isolation valve and control valve

Water exits the control valve via one-and-a-half-inch iron pipework discharging into the pit. A clayware drain travels underground to the turbine pit. Much of the original drain pipework had corroded away.

Control Valve

The hoist is controlled by a three-position bobbin valve which is used to raise, lower or stop the piston. The valve body is a bronze casting apart from one flange which is cast-iron and screwed to the main body.

In the 'raise' and 'lower' positions the valve directs water to one side of the piston or the other, allowing water on the opposite side of the piston to be drained away.

The gland in the hoist control valve was found to be packed with greased string; this is now replaced with modern, quarter-inch packing. The control valve was found to stick in some situations because of a misalignment between the top of the valve and the gland follower, the studs of which were found to be bent. The follower was evidently not concentric with the shaft.

New studs were made and a small amount of metal removed from the follower. This follower appears never to have fitted properly (nor, in fact, does the piston-rod gland follower, which is now similarly repaired). The vertical control rod was straightened during restoration. The rod had been originally joined to the control valve by a fitting forged from the end of the rod; the rod-end was drilled to allow a set-bolt to be fastened through it, via a corresponding hole in the end of the valve spindle.

In order to disconnect the rod from the control valve the rod had to be cut off. The components were subsequently welded back together.

During operation, when the valve is in the 'raise' position water is directed to the top of the cylinder, forcing the piston downwards. The lifting chain travels over the pulley, raising the sacks. When the valve is in the 'lower' position water is directed to the base of the cylinder, forcing the piston upwards, lowering the chain. In the 'stop' position the water on both sides of the piston is 'locked in', preventing the piston from moving in either direction.

The hoist control valve does not appear to have had rubber seals. Instead, in a similar fashion to the main hoist piston, each of the two control valve pistons has a series of half-round grooves machined in it at approximately quarter-inch centres.

Operating Mechanism

The hoist operating mechanism uses a vertical rod to link the control valve in the pit to a lever on the first floor.

The lever is mounted horizontally on the floor inside a wooden compartment with a removable lid, made from tongue-and-groove boarding. It is weighted down with a lead block and is operated by a chain connected to one end of it.

The chain travels over pulleys before terminating in a steel strap, with a handle at one end, that can be hung on a pin mounted on the wall.

The steel handle on the first-floor wall that is used to raise, lower or stop the hoist

The strap can be fastened in any of three positions—these correspond to the 'raise', 'lower' and 'stop' positions of the hoist control valve. ('Raise' is the strap's lowest position.)

The lever compartment was in good condition despite containing a considerable amount of organic debris. It also contained some items of cast iron that could not be identified but which may have once been used in place of, or in addition to, the lead weight on the lever. During restoration the compartment was cleaned out and the old metal weights retained.

A length of iron rod with hooks at each end is used to 'hook' the sacks of grain and pull them to one side of the hatch in the floor. From there they could be safely lowered to the floor and taken to the Granary. The rod was found nearby, undisturbed since the last time the hoist was used in the nineteen-fifties.

The operating chain and lever, which had become disconnected due to corrosion, were reconnected by cutting open the end link of the chain and welding it back together.

Operating the Hoist

The photographic sequence below shows the hydraulic hoist raising a sack of grain from the ground-floor cart shed to the first-floor Granary landing area.

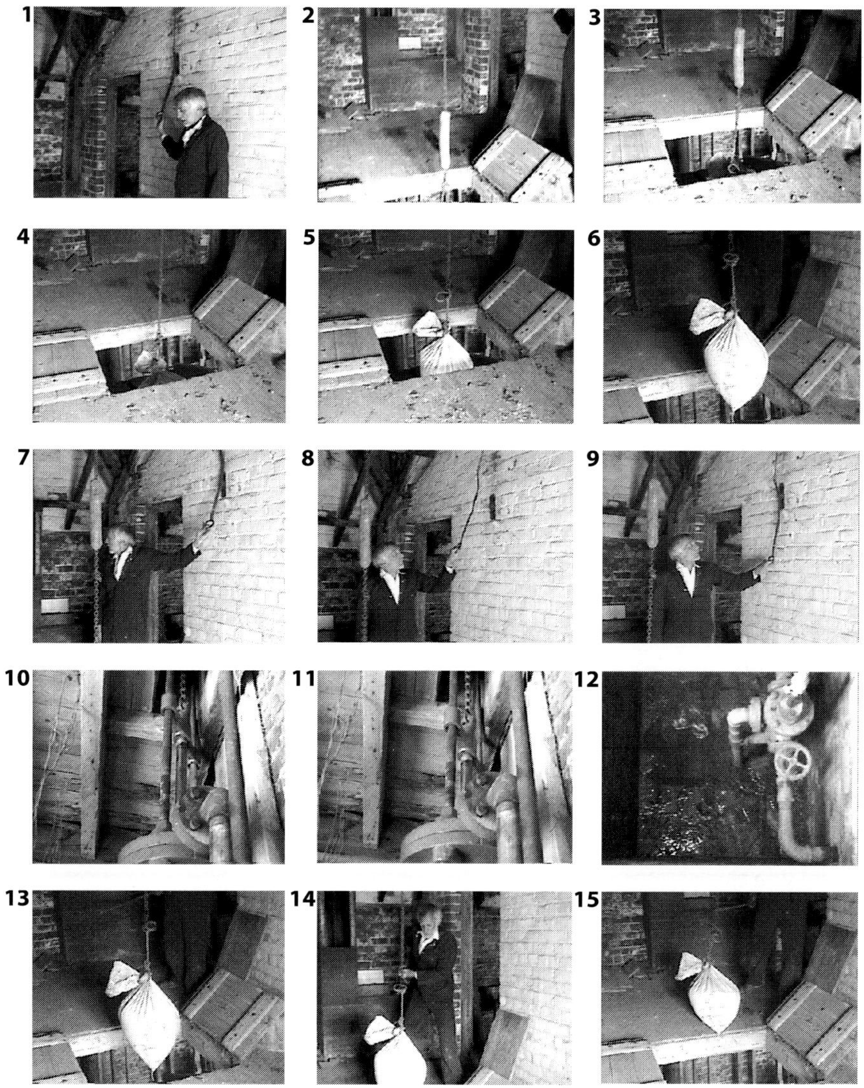

A series of stills taken from a video of the hoist being tested in 2001 (filmed by Ian Wilson)

The film sequence shown here is taken from a short video filmed in 2001 soon after the hoist was restored. The hoist performed admirably, despite its age, and was brought back to full working order for the first time in fifty years.

1 The steel strap is locked in the 'raise' position, opening the valve and directing water into the top of the cylinder. This forces the piston down, pulling the chain over the pulley and raising the lifting chain and hook.

2 The chain and hook connected to the grain sack begin their ascent from the ground-floor cart shed towards the open trapdoor in the ceiling above.

3 The lead counterbalance is now clearly in view as the chain continues to rise at a rate of several inches per second.

4 The chain has taken up the slack and is now lifting the grain sack.

5 The counterbalance has passed out of view as the chain continues its travel towards the pulley in the first-floor ceiling.

6 The grain sack is now at first-floor level—the whole operation so far has taken approximately 30 seconds.

7 The steel strap is locked in the 'stop' position while the operator checks that the sack is clear of the trapdoor.

8 More height is required so the steel strap is adjusted to raise the sack a little higher.

9 The sack is fully clear of the trapdoor; the operator puts the strap in the 'stop' position to prevent the chain rising any higher.

10 This view shows the top of the cylinder, just below the ground-floor ceiling, immediately before the operator raises the sack in picture **8**. The piston is already near the end of its downward travel.

11 The vertical control rod (farthest right) has been raised by the operator using the strap in picture **8**. This rod opens the control valve, forcing water on top of the piston, which now reaches its lower position.

12 Inside the valve pit water is pushed out of the drain pipe at the bottom of the control valve by the piston on its downward stroke.

13 Back on the first floor, a hook-ended iron rod is used to grab the chain and pull the grain sack away from the trapdoor.

14 The sack is dragged onto the solid floor ready to be taken to the Granary.

15 Water leakage past the piston means that a parked sack will gradually descend—but this descent is only at the rate of about one inch per second.

Architectural Notes

The precise age of the hoist building is unrecorded. The cart sheds near the road were built in 1826 but the 1856 Ordnance Survey map shows that these originally stood alone.

More stone buildings were added in 1874 but it was not until 1880 that the brick wings forming the 'E'-range were added. It is at this time that the cart sheds are believed to have been linked up with the Granary building.

The hoist was installed in 1881 in a cart shed—it is not known whether this was adapted from an existing shed or purpose-built for the hoist. There are two theories...

A specially constructed dormer roof houses the top pulley of the hoist. This construction exhibits late-Victorian features and appears to be contemporary with the hoist. This favours the 'purpose-built' theory.

However, during restoration, some timber between the courses of bricks in the upper first-floor was thought to indicate that the gable end may have been added later for the hoist.

Further evidence to support the 'adaptation' theory came from the ground floor: the wall behind the mounting board was whitewashed, indicating that the building was in use before the hoist was installed.

Exterior gable end showing the specially constructed roof accommodating the hoist

The hoist and mounting board had been painted with blue–grey gloss in the nineteen-thirties and some of this remained prior to restoration. No older paint layers were found. Below ground there is hardly any evidence of paint. There was no paint on the operating mechanism. The wooden lever-compartment on the first-floor had a matt paint finish.

A Recent Discovery...

The name W G Armstrong appears in many references to J W Pease and the Hutton Estate. Armstrong's engineering works at Elswick, Newcastle-upon-Tyne built and supplied many water-driven machines including, it is believed, the Home Farm hydraulic hoist. A recent discovery provides further evidence that there was a strong connection between Pease and Armstrong.

In the Armstrong archive collection at Blandford Square, Newcastle-upon-Tyne, document number 1138 depicts a three-cylinder hydraulic engine which was designed for J W Pease Esq. of Hutton Hall. This document is an engineering drawing dated 10/4/72, five years after Hutton Hall was built.

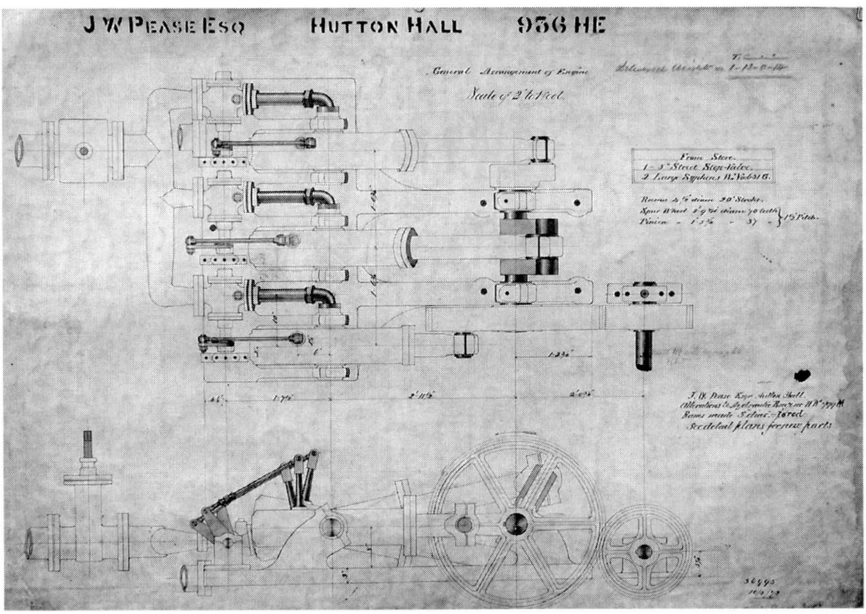

Drawing of a three-cylinder hydraulic engine built in 1872 for J W Pease Esq., Hutton Hall. Drawing discovered by J K Harrison in September 2005 and reproduced courtesy of Tyne & Wear Archives Service (reference: 1027/1138)

The existence of this drawing shows that Pease and Armstrong were known to each other in the early eighteen-seventies, thus increasing the likelihood that the Farm's hydraulic hoist was manufactured in the Elswick Works.

Hydraulic engines such as the one described here were sometimes used to power lifts in large houses, but there is no evidence that such a lift was installed in Hutton Hall.

Nevertheless there are indications that the hydraulic engine was built: the drawing has been edited and some of the components have been modified. The notes would imply that alterations were made to an existing engine not a proposed one...

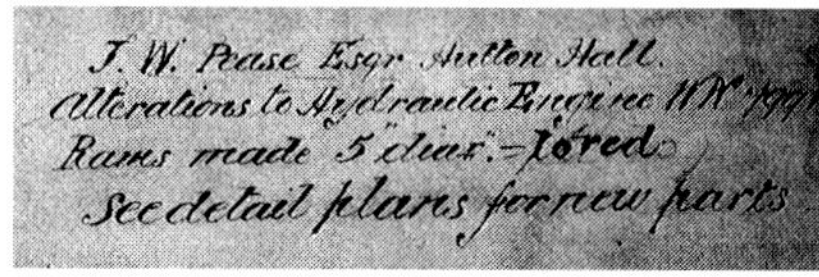

An excerpt from the Armstrong drawing noting 'Alterations to Hydraulic Engine...'

...but the ground plan of Hutton Hall has no reference to an 'engine'.

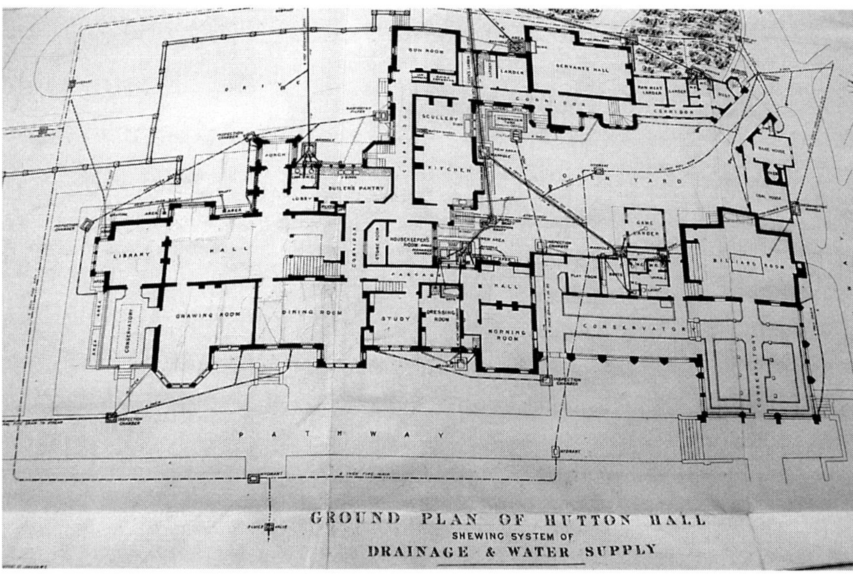

An OME archive 'Ground Plan of Hutton Hall shewing system of Drainage & Water Supply'

An 1871 Armstrong drawing in the OME collection proposes a water pipeline between Bold Venture Gill and Home Farm, and an undated letter acknowledges the delivery of pipework—including enough six-inch pipe to cover a distance of over six hundred yards. It is not known whether this was contemporary with the engine. (The Blue Lake supply uses nine-, eight-, seven- and two-inch diameter pipe, but not six-inch.)

Hydraulic engines were used in many nineteenth-century installations but few survive. Some remaining examples can be seen in Newcastle's swing bridge, London's Tower Bridge, and in the Armstrong Museum at Bamburgh Castle in Northumberland.

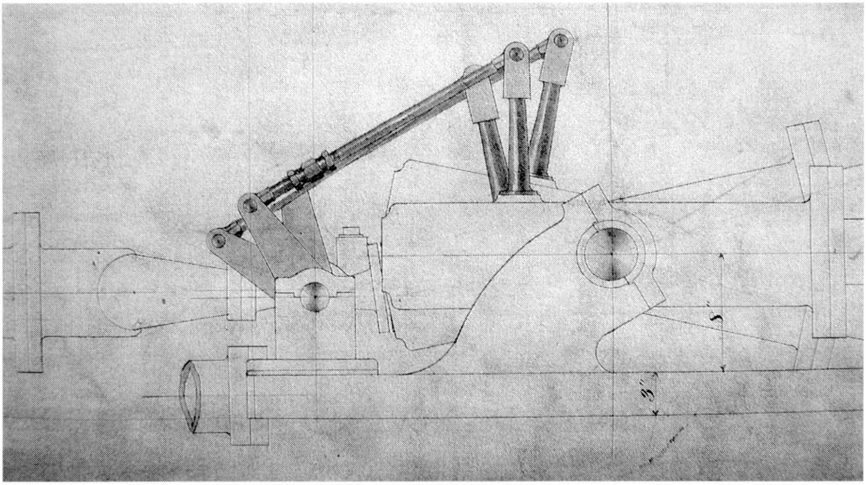

The left-hand side of the Armstrong hydraulic engine showing the cylinders

The right-hand side of the Armstrong hydraulic engine showing the drive wheel

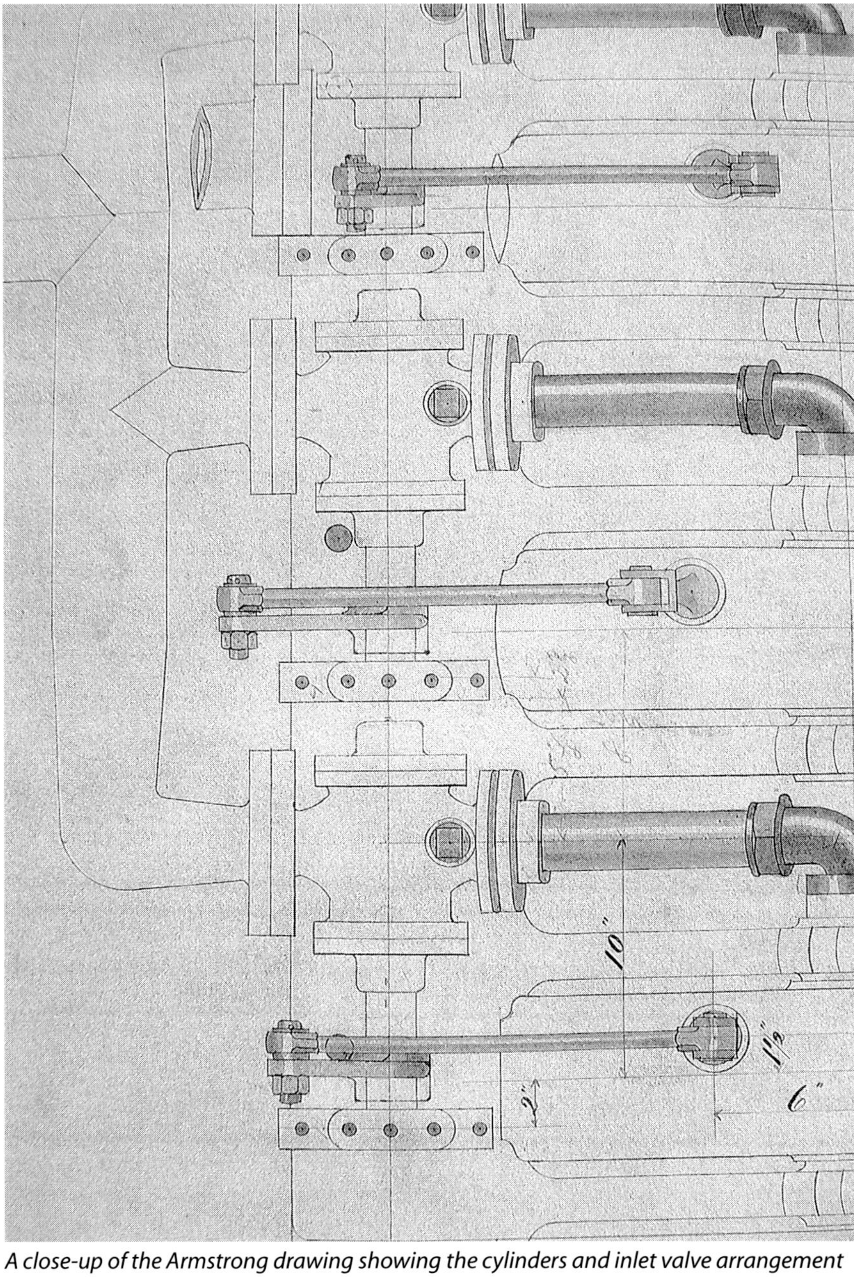

A close-up of the Armstrong drawing showing the cylinders and inlet valve arrangement

Chapter 8

Home Farm Machinery

List of Machinery

Joinery	two circular-saw benches
	mortising machine
	band saw
	centre lathe
	grindstone
	planer (a later addition)
Granary	grain mill
	oat crusher
	oil-seed-cake breaker
	straw cutter
	turnip chopper
	bone mill

NOTE: Wood panelling is fitted in the Granary turbine shed between the door and the wall; this covers a slot that allowed a drive-belt from the main turbine drive-shaft to power a bone mill located outside the turbine shed. An additional (now bricked-up) slot in the wall of the nearby electricity Generator house also lines up with the panelling, suggesting that either the bone mill could be powered by the generator's steam engine or that the steam engine could be used to drive the main turbine shaft—and therefore the Granary machinery—when there was insufficient water in Blue Lake.

Previous page: *Barn machinery in the first-floor workshop next to the Granary. This was powered by drive belts connected to the lineshaft (top left). The lineshaft was driven by a belt connected to the drive-shaft pulley on the ground-floor turbine. This photograph was taken in December 2004, shortly before redevelopment began. The machinery had been recently restored by the Home Farm Hydraulic Machinery Restoration Group*

Home Farm Machinery

Mechanisation

The aim of the hydraulic installation was to mechanise everyday farming tasks which were difficult, slow and labour-intensive. The installation of the Granary turbine and hydraulic hoist reduced the physical effort involved in lifting grain bags, making fertiliser and animal feed, grinding cereal and cutting straw.

The Joinery turbine supplied power to a range of woodworking equipment, thus enabling repairs and construction work on the Estate.

Inside the first-floor Granary workshop

The Joinery Workshop containing the basement turbine and ground-floor machinery

Granary

The Granary turbine powered a lineshaft in the workshop above. Drive-belts were used to connect pulleys along the lineshaft to the barn machinery.

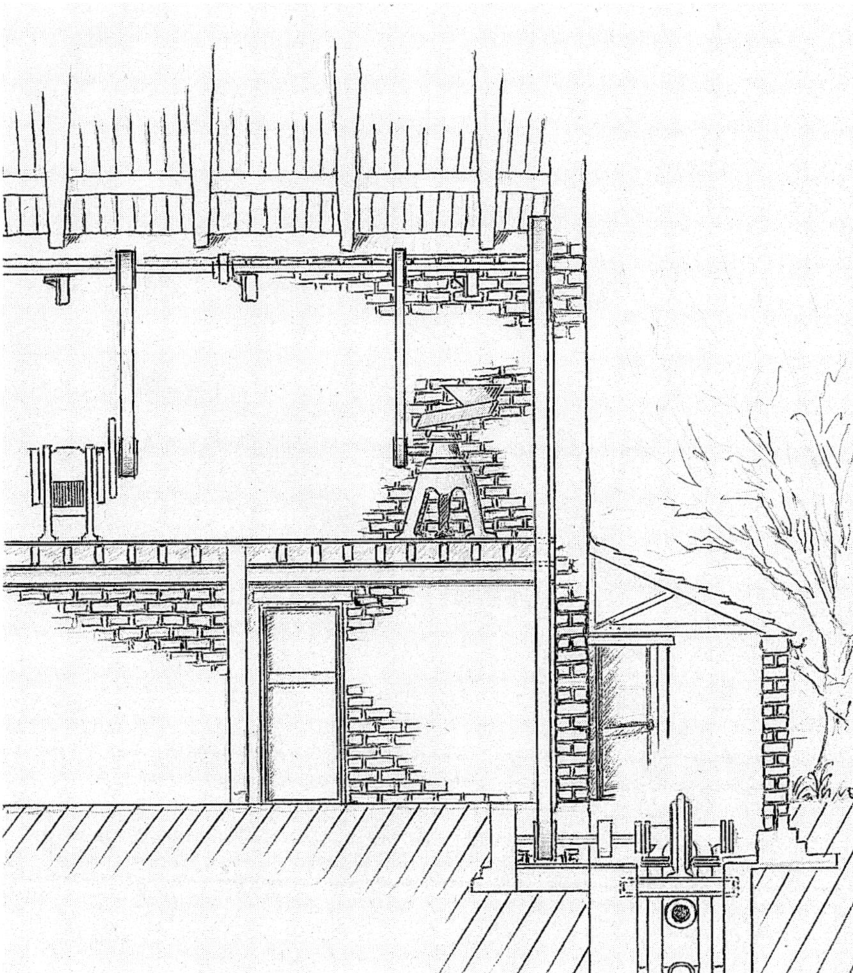

Cross-sectional view of the Granary turbine shed and first-floor barn machinery. Prepared by J K Harrison from the original drawing in the Cleveland Archives ('Arrangement of 6 HP Turbine and farm machinery for Hutton Grange, Williamson Bros., Kendal'), and used to illustrate ***Hydraulic machinery at Hutton Home Farm near Guisborough, The Cleveland Industrial Archaeologist****, No. 25 (1998), p29–42. Adapted here by Ian Brown*

Pulley wheel on the first-floor lineshaft with drive-belt connected to the Granary turbine

The photograph above shows the first-floor workshop with the drive-belt rising from the turbine below.

The lineshaft stretches the full length of the workshop and was used to supply power to numerous machines located along its length, via pulley-wheels every few yards.

The cross-shaped bracket beneath the window once supported a speed control mechanism. This connected to the turbine guide blades via an iron rod fastened to the outside of the wall. The rod entered the shed roof and terminated in a rack-and-pinion arrangement at the turbine.

Turbine control rod rising to the workshop

Joinery Workshop

The Joinery Workshop turbine is located in the basement and is accessible by a short wooden ladder. The turbine drove a lineshaft on the ground floor via a belt and pulley system. The ground-floor lineshaft supplied power to the saws and other woodworking machinery by a system of belts and pulleys.

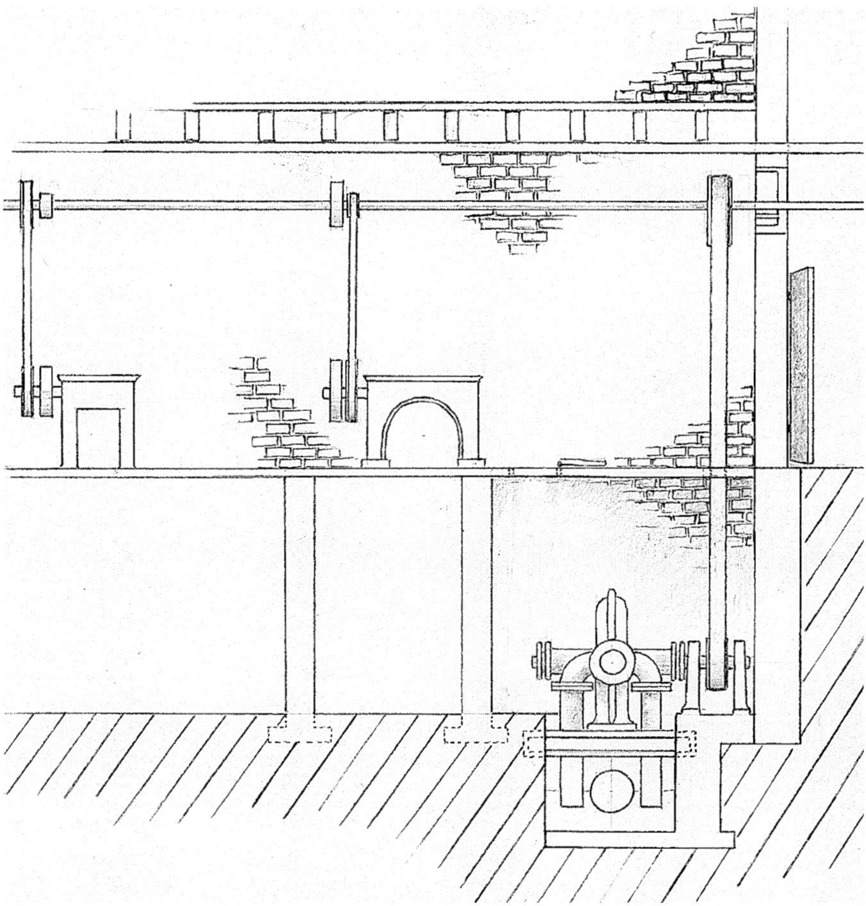

Cross-sectional view of the basement turbine and ground-floor machinery. Prepared by J K Harrison from the original drawing in the Cleveland Archives ('Arrangement of 7 HP Turbine and farm machinery for Hutton Grange, Williamson Bros., Kendal'), and used to illustrate ***Hydraulic machinery at Hutton Home Farm near Guisborough, The Cleveland Industrial Archaeologist****, No. 25 (1998), p29–42. Adapted here by Ian Brown*

The lineshaft in the Joinery Workshop showing some of the drive pulleys, including a three-speed stepped pulley (photograph by Jim Prentice)

Circular-saw bench made by A. Ransome and Co. of Chelsea, London (Clive Wilson)

Close-up views of the circular-saw bench (photographs by Jim Prentice)

Underside of a 36-inch circular-saw bench showing the drive-belt slot (Clive Wilson)

The planing machine (Jim Prentice)

The Estate Workshops

The 1903 sale documents for the Hutton Hall Estate describe the Joinery Workshop in its original condition:

> *'Near to are timber and tile-built, and comprise Two Bay Timber Store Shed, Paintshop Lath Room; Sawing Shed fitted with sliding doors, with Joiner's Shop over; Store House; Blacksmith's Shop and Shoeing Shed with Store Room over, Turbine House in basement approached by trap door, from which power is obtained for driving the saw benches and other machinery.'*

The Workshop has survived for over one hundred years without any significant changes. The turbine and its pipework are intact and much of the original machinery still exists.

The building itself is Grade II-listed.

End view of the Joinery Workshop, 2005

Chapter 9

Blue Lake Restoration

Diary of Events

September 2004	the bypass channel is reinstated around the Lake's perimeter one thousand cubic metres of silt is dug out and removed
October 2004	the sluice valve is excavated and taken away for repair the drain-valve pit is dug out and the drain valve removed
November 2004	the dam and weir are excavated to expose the original walls the dam retaining walls are rebuilt using reclaimed stone
December 2004	loose stone is salvaged from the eroded spillway channel the stilling pond walls and base are dismantled and rebuilt
January 2005	brick and stone walls are remade along either side of the weir clay is firmly packed under the weir slab and nearby cavities
February 2005	loose bricks and mortar are removed from the spillway base the eroded spillway channel is cleared out ready for clay infill
March 2005	concrete extension is cast alongside the horizontal weir stone clay is firmly packed in the gap between the two dam walls
April 2005	machinery is brought on site to refill the spillway with clay the clay on the dam and spillway is compacted and profiled
May 2005	the stone weir base and brick walls are widened and raised machinery is used to level the dam and landscape the area
June 2005	the clay in the spillway channel is measured and levelled off wooden shuttering is fitted ready for the new concrete
July 2005	concrete is dry-mixed and laid on the surface of the spillway concrete is tamped and profiled to match the original pattern
August 2005	the spillway channels are prepared for the final brickwork brick walls are begun on either side of the concrete spillway
September 2005	brickwork continues downwards towards the stilling pond the area around the spillway is repaired and landscaped
October 2005	the brick walls along the edges of the spillway are complete new vertical wooden pillars and control rods are designed
November 2005	the sluice and drain valves are prepared for reassembly strainers are designed to prevent debris entering the valves

Previous page: *Volunteers digging out silt from around the drain valve in October 2004. This was a difficult operation requiring a 'human chain'—workers in the valve pit would fill a bucket, which was then hauled up on a rope and emptied into a barrow on the dam*

Blue Lake Restoration

Dereliction and Decay

Blue Lake remained intact until the late nineteen-fifties when the pier was damaged by forestry operations. A decade later the pier was still in place but the wooden cross-pieces had gone—only one horizontal timber remained between the vertical pillars and the bankside.

The water supply to Home Farm no longer functioned and the turbines and hoist fell into disuse.

All through the nineteen-seventies and nineteen-eighties the Lake continued to deteriorate with silt increasing year-by-year. The weather caused further damage and at some point the dam was breached during a storm: much of the stonework was washed away downstream and the concrete spillway collapsed.

By 2001 Blue Lake was no longer a lake. It wasn't very blue either.

By 2001 Blue Lake appeared to be in terminal decline, with the valves buried under twelve feet of silt and vegetation surrounding the remains of the two vertical wooden pillars

By 2001 the sediment had reached the full height of the weir and the retaining walls of the dam had long since been washed into the stream.

With the walls breached there was nothing to hold back the water. The spillway was gradually eroded until it became a deep fissure in the clay.

View across the derelict Lake, looking towards the track

View from the track across to the weir and spillway

Clearing and Dredging

In September 2004 the dredging contractors arrived on site and the footpaths were sealed off.

The contractors were supervised on site by volunteer members of the Blue Lake Restoration Group.

Land & Water Plant Ltd., the dredging contractors, arrive on site

Preparing a clearing for the silt (Eric Ward)

The dredging operation begins (Eric Ward)

Having found a suitable place to spread the silt the contractors began clearing the Lake of trees and debris.

To keep the bed of Blue Lake dry enough for dredging to proceed safely the original bypass channel had to be brought back into use.

The section of the bypass channel in the forest was completely blocked and had to be dug out for a distance of about three hundred feet, to join the original concrete and brick section which emerges from the trees close to the weir.

When the bypass channel was dredged the fall of its bed was decided by the flow of water which occurred as the digging took place. The channel was reinstated above the lake and the stream entering the lake was then dammed with timber.

The reinstated bypass channel that directs water around the perimeter of the Lake

Digging the bypass channel (by Eric Ward)

With the stream safely diverted it was now time to dig out the Lake itself. The excavation had to be deep enough to remove the silt, but not so deep as to damage the original clay lining in the bed of the Lake. This turned out to be a delicate balance.

The depth of excavation had been estimated some months earlier when the Lake was surveyed using scaffold poles driven into the silt.

This depth was estimated to be about twelve feet below the overflow level of the weir.

Eventually more than a thousand cubic metres of silt was dug out and deposited on the cleared forestry on the opposite side of the track.

The sides of the Lake had been thought to be cobbled but this turned out not to be so—although parts of the dam were brick-lined.

The empty Lake soon after dredging

Dredging the Lake (photo by Eric Ward)

Dredging was a tricky operation: no-one knew the exact shape of the Lake. As the machinery dug deeper it was important not to puncture the clay lining—this lining is an essential feature installed by the original dam builders to ensure that the water did not leak away. Scraping away the silt from the lower levels required a steady, methodical approach.

As the dredger's bucket closed in on the dam there was an additional concern—the valves and control rods were buried deep under the silt. To prevent damage it was decided to leave this section to the volunteers.

Diversions and Deflectors

A section of the cast-iron supply pipe to Home Farm was broken into just below the dam and a blanking plate fitted. A short diversion pipe was used to direct water into the stream.

Temporary diversion pipe fitted to the main water supply pipe to Home Farm

Water exiting the temporary diversion pipe

The main sluice valve was then dug out, dismantled and removed. This allowed water to flow through the dam and back into the stream via the temporary diversion pipe.

This arrangement allowed any water collecting in the Lake to be fed away safely downstream.

The bypass channel at the top of the Lake would have originally had a deflector to direct water either into the Lake or around the channel into the stilling pond. There are no visible remains of this deflector but some low, crescent-shaped brick walls have been discovered nearby. These may be part of a deflector system.

Brick walls in the vicinity of the deflector

A new wooden deflector gate was built during the restoration works.

Wooden deflector gate built in 2004

Sluice and Drain Valves

The dredger was unable to remove silt from a small area near the dam so this was later dug out by hand.

Volunteers digging out the valve pits...

The operating spindle for the main valve was missing and could not be found in the area around the valve.

...and searching for missing components

The remainder of the silt covering the valves was dug out, bucketed to the top of the dam and taken away.

The drain valve is uncovered at last

Fortunately the spindle for the drain valve was still in position—but required a lot of effort to remove it.

Attempting to remove the valve spindle

Separating the spindle from the valve top

The sluice valve was the first to be dug out—this had to be opened so that water flowing into the Lake could be directed away through the temporary pipe into the stream.

The control rod and its mechanism were missing and could not be found in the silt. Fortunately the larger components had survived and the sluice valve box was intact.

The brick face of the dam showing the sluice-valve box on the right and the drain-valve pit on the left. Metal strainers would have covered both apertures when the dam was built

View of the inside of the sluice-valve box

The cast-iron sluice-valve box showing the integral water pipe supplying Home Farm

When the sluice valve was removed the water flowed down the pipe and into the stream. It was now time to remove the drain valve.

After much digging the top of the drain valve was exposed. The gland-follower nuts turned freely after an initial tap with a hammer and chisel. The gland packing was authentic: horse-hair impregnated with grease.

The spindle was seized within the valve top so it was necessary to remove the four cover-bolts and turn the whole valve-top with a wrench in order to open the valve.

The gate was successfully opened by this method and water flowed freely through the valve. The inflowing water was used to clear the remaining silt from the pit.

The drain-valve pit from the front showing the strainer box and gate valve (tops removed)

Removing the iron control rod proved to be more difficult; attempts to lift both this and the internal part of the valve while joined together proved futile. An attempt was made to 'unscrew' the rod from the gate, which was successful, but the gate then proved impossible to extricate. At one point the gate dropped back inside the valve and the valve closed;

unfortunately by this time the water had been diverted into the drain pit which rapidly began to fill up.

Three volunteers frantically tried to screw the spindle back into the valve, finally succeeding to reopen the valve. They then decided to use the control rod as a slide hammer—pulling it upwards with a sharp tug. Thankfully this managed to shear the scroll pin from the control rod and separate the two components.

The gate lifted out by hand and the water flowed away. If the pit had filled up the valve would have been submerged under four feet of water.

View from inside the drain valve pit, with water coming in from the Lake

Both the drain valve and strainer are in good condition despite being under water for a hundred years. This could be due to their being completely entombed in several feet of organic sediment. The valve is now restored and reused, although the strainer will be replaced.

The strainer has corroded in places and would need some repair work. It also struggled to cope with the debris and sediment encountered during the restoration work. A larger, more robust strainer and filter system is being installed as part of the restoration project.

The following photographs show the valve components in detail.

The drain-valve pit viewed from above

Drain valve spindle and gland, dismantled, showing the original horse-hair packing

Valve spindle (scroll-pin hole visible in top)

This cast-iron 'gate' slides inside the valve body. The threaded end of the spindle is held in the recess by a retainer (see below)

Buried Treasure

During hand-digging operations many bottles and jars were found. The oldest one, a clear glass mineral water by Harper in Stockton from about 1900, was found at the deepest point of the Lake: in the base of the drain valve pit.

Many other miscellaneous items were retrieved from the sediment—including several glass marbles, a 1940 Army stainless-steel table knife, a toy boat and a couple of toy cars, two old coins, a piece of jet, and a sachet of Bob Martin dog shampoo.

Treasure found in the mud: five marbles, a plastic VW transporter, bottle stoppers, jam jars, a 1940 Army knife, unused 'Show-Ring' dog shampoo, a piece of jet, two halfpenny pieces from 1955 and 1959, a third-of-a-pint milk bottle, a beer bottle from Tower Ale Felling-on-Tyne, Horlicks jars and assorted bottles from Northern Dairies, Lowcocks, Garnets, Cinzano, Schweppes, Tizer, Danish Lager, Espiner Loftus, and EN Jones of Bishop Auckland

Some of the missing ironwork and valve controls were found deep in the silt. Parts of the strainers were discovered but these had mostly corroded and fallen to pieces, apart from one section that was intact.

Various bolts and brackets were found; these helped to build up a picture of the original design. They included a 'U'-shaped bracket that once fastened the crosspiece to the tops of the vertical pier supports.

A cast-iron strainer rescued from the silt

A bracket from one of the pier supports

A close-up view of the cast-iron strainer

Markings on the face of a rescued timber

Stilling Pond

The stilling pond had suffered as a result of the spillway- and dam-collapse and much of the loose material had ended up falling into it. During restoration the debris was cleared out and the outflow pipe from the drain valve brought back into use. The pond walls were in poor condition and had to be rebuilt.

The stilling pond wall shortly before reconstruction began

Rebuilding the stilling pond wall. The stones were numbered before being removed and reinstated

The stilling pond during reconstruction

The stone walls were dismantled and reconstructed, mortar being used for the first few (lower) courses. Upper courses were laid without mortar.

The base of the pond was re-laid using large boulders wedged tightly together. This is how the pond had been made but over the years some of the boulders had washed out.

A layer of gravel from the stream was added to fill the remaining gaps.

The photograph on the left shows the reconstruction phase; the photo below shows the finished pond with water flowing in from the Lake.

Reconstruction is complete; water is entering the pond through the drain-valve outflow

Weir and Dam

The weir had been raised eighteen inches above its original height by the addition of a concrete ledge, some years after it was first built.

This had lifted the water level which in turn had increased the erosion along the front of the dam.

During restoration this ledge was removed to reveal a wide, sloping slab made of dressed sandstone.

View from the derelict weir to the track

The weir and its 'modern' concrete ledge—evidently built to raise the water level

Excavating the foundations of the walls

The concrete ledge during demolition

Preparing to rebuild the dam walls

The dam walls in the vicinity of the weir had been washed away and the surrounding area was badly eroded. These walls were rebuilt using local reclaimed stone and the cavity was filled with compacted yellow clay.

The dam walls during reconstruction

The cavity partly filled with yellow clay...

The weir was widened and raised to comply with modern regulations.

Preparing to extend the weir with concrete

Ramming clay underneath the weir slab...

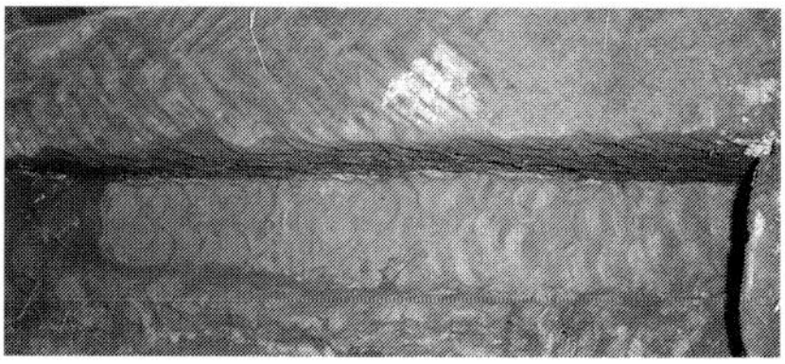

...creating a water-tight seal

Spillway Channel

The spillway from the weir to the pond originally had brick sides and a concrete base. One side and part of the base remained but the other side had long since been washed away.

The collapsed spillway seen from below

The collapsed spillway seen from above

During restoration the fissure was filled with clay and compacted, the concrete base renewed and the brick walls repaired and rebuilt.

Repairing the base was a difficult task because of the steep slope of the spillway: a semi-dry concrete mix had to be used in order to reduce the risk of the concrete 'slumping'.

Reinstating the spillway with new clay

Compacting the clay in the spillway

Mixing semi-dry concrete for the spillway

Profiling and compacting the concrete

The spillway finally begins to take shape

Finished at Last...(nearly)

By November 2005 the volunteers had levelled the dam and rebuilt the brick walls that run along the edges of the spillway. At the time of writing plans are being drawn up for the last big task—the replacement of the sluice and drain valves and the structure that supported them. Blue Lake will soon rise again.

Index

Bibliography

The following sources provide additional information on many of the subjects in this book.

Hydraulic machinery at Hutton Home Farm near Guisborough*, The Cleveland Industrial Archaeologist, No. 25 (1998), p29–42, John K Harrison*

Two Ancient Townships, Studies of Pinchinthorpe and Hutton Lowcross*, Grace Dixon*

Religion, Business and Society in North-East England: The Pease Family of Darlington in the Nineteenth Century*, Anne Orde, 2000*

On the Development of Water Power*, Gilbert Gilkes & Co., Ltd., 1903*

Guisborough Before 1900*, B J D Harrison and G Dixon, 1994*

Hutton Lowcross in the 1940's and 1950's*, Pam Wilson, 2003*

Drainage of Hutton Hall Guisborough and Other Buildings on the Hutton Estate, 1884–5*, Teesside Archives OME collection (see also other documents in the OME collection)*

Teesside's Economic Heritage*, G A North, 1975*

A Century in Stone, The Eston and California Story *(DVD), Craig Hornby, 2005*

Whitby Jet Through the Years*, Mabel McMillan, 1992*

Eight Centuries of Milling in North East Yorkshire*, John K Harrison, 2001*

Home Farm & Hutton Hall Appraisal*, North York Moors National Park Authority*